I0083132

Burial Records of Four
Grant County
Indiana
Quaker Cemeteries

Ralph D. Kirkpatrick

HERITAGE BOOKS
2012

HERITAGE BOOKS

AN IMPRINT OF HERITAGE BOOKS, INC.

Books, CDs, and more—Worldwide

For our listing of thousands of titles see our website
at
www.HeritageBooks.com

Published 2012 by
HERITAGE BOOKS, INC.
Publishing Division
100 Railroad Ave. #104
Westminster, Maryland 21157

Copyright © 1999 Ralph D. Kirkpatrick

All rights reserved. No part of this book may be reproduced or
transmitted in any form or by any means, electronic or mechanical,
including photocopying, recording or by any information storage
and retrieval system without written permission from the author,
except for the inclusion of brief quotations in a review.

International Standard Book Numbers
Paperbound: 978-0-7884-1118-2
Clothbound: 978-0-7884-8993-8

TABLE OF CONTENTS

Foreword   v

Abbreviations and Conventions   vii

Mississinewa Friends Cemetery   1

Deer Creek Friends Cemetery   91

Little Ridge Friends Cemetery   101

Oak Ridge Friends Cemetery   111

Key to Documentation   129

Maiden Name Index   135

iii

FOREWORD

We know our spouse and our children and, in most instances, we know our parents. But who were our great-grandparents? Who built and lived in the older house that we now rent or own? Who was the pioneer that cut away the forest to create the local farm fields? Who tilled the soil in the farm field that is now occupied by our subdivision? Were they born here or did they migrate here from another state or country? Were these people married? Did they worship where we now worship? What were their surnames? Were they of similar ethnic origin as the people we now know in our subdivision?

We may wander through local cemeteries and read names and dates on gravestones. The stones sometimes tantalize us with a fraternal or military symbol. They may be carved into the likeness of a lamb or angel but are otherwise mute about the person whose life they are meant to memorialize. We are sometimes frustrated in finding what is obviously a grave but the marker is blank or is eroded into illegibility or only consists of initials such as 'A. R.' or 'P. K.'

This volume is a small attempt to help identify and 'flesh out' some of the lives of persons buried in four of the five 19th century Quaker cemeteries located in Grant County, Indiana.

Ralph D. Kirkpatrick, Ph.D.
Osage Farm

ABBREVIATIONS AND CONVENTIONS

b - date of birth
bur - buried at
ca - circa or about
Cem - Cemetery
ch - child of or children of
Ch. - Church
Coll - College
Co. - county name; if not followed by a state name is an
    Indiana county
CW - Civil War
d - died or died on
dec - deceased
dt - daughter of
f - former or formerly
grad - graduate or graduate of
m - married
mbr - member of
M.E. - Methodist Episcopal
MH - Meetinghouse; building used by Friends for religious
    services; is in Indiana if not followed by a State name
MM - Monthly Meeting; conducts the business of a local
    group of Friends; MM not followed by a state name is
    in Indiana
M & M - Mr. and Mrs.
Normal - educational institution training teachers
prob - probably
(Name) - maiden surname of married woman or widow
'Name' - nickname
Name - name this person was known by or 'went by'
Recorded Friends Minister - formally recognized by Friends
    as a Minister of the Gospel
s - son of
serv - served in or served as
tchr - teacher
Twp. - Township; township name not followed by a county
    name is in Grant County, Indiana
U.B. - United Brethren Church

Mississinewa Friends Cemetery was established on the John Ballinger farm on the south side of the Mississinewa River by the Mississinewa Monthly Meeting of Friends near their meetinghouse. It is located in Marion adjacent to the east side of Lincoln Boulevard just south of its junction with Pennsylvania Avenue. This burial ground is smaller than two acres and is in the W half of the SE quarter of Section 8, Township 24N, Range 8E, Center Township, Grant County, Indiana. The Friends sold it to the local IOOF Lodge in 1861. The IOOF Lodge added acreage to the cemetery until it now includes 108 acres. It was sold by the IOOF in 1989 to a private group who now calls the cemetery 'Estates of Serenity.' Burials continue to occur in the non-Friends portion of the cemetery.

ADAMSON, Claude M. - b 13 Oct 1889; s John C. and Rachel A. Adamson; d 11 Nov 1898 or ca 20 May 1896 (29,37)

ADAMSON, John C. - b 1857; m Rachel Ann; d ca 28 Mar 1947 (29,37)

ADAMSON, Rachel Ann - b 1861; m John C. Adamson; d ca 29 Jan or Jun 1936 (29,37)

ADAMSON, Samuel - non-Friend; d 1827 or before, first person bur in this cem (27)

ADKINS, __ - d 15 Jan 1873 (29)

ADKINS, Frank W. - b 11 Apr 1861; d 12 Sep 1875 (29)

ADKINS, Leotter M. - b 11 May 1863; d 15 Apr 1875 (29)

ADKINS, Mattie - b 11 Nov 1833; m Dr. J.C. Adkins; d 24 Jan 1877 (29,73)

ALLEN, Jane - b Grant Co. 9 Sep 1836; dt William and Sarah (Symons) Allen; mbr Mississinewa MM; d 20 Aug 1837 (1,25, 29,46,65)

ALSUP, Jeffery E. - b 27 Dec 1961; d 6 Apr 1991 (29)

ANDREW, Hannah J. - b OH 21 Jan 1852; dt Stanton and Mary Andrew; d 16 Jul 1869 (29,50)

ANDREW, Levi T. - b 13 Dec 1841; s John Andrew; d 7 Jun 1850 (29)

ANDREW, Mary - b OH 9 Jun 1800; m Stanton Andrew; d 18 Feb 1861 (29,50)

ANDREW, Rachel - (29)

ANDREW, Robert - b NC 11 Feb 1782; prob s William and Hannah Andrew; m Ellen Faulkner prior to Oct 1807; mbr Mississinewa MM; d 1 Feb 1856 (1,17,24,29,30,65)

ANDREWS, Ellen - d ca 19 Jan 1917 (29,37)

ARNETT, Levi A. - b NC 30 Nov 1824; m Hannah Andrews 25 Feb 1858; d 13 Dec 1877 (10,27,29,50,54)

ARNOLD, Jeremiah - b NC 9 Aug 1805; s Nathan and Elizabeth (Horn) Arnold; 20 Jan 1836 m Elizabeth Symonds; mbr Mississinewa MM; d 30 Jul 1852 (1,17,65)

BAKER, Laura (Frazzee) - 7 Dec 1892 m Clyde Baker; d 25 Jul 1895 at age 23 (12,16,29,37,47)

BALDWIN, Addison M. - b Fairmount Twp. 1 Aug 1841; s Thomas and Lydia (Thomas) Baldwin; 1st m 10 Aug 1865 Aladelpha 'Allie' Jones (dec 8 Nov 1883); 2nd m Mrs. Kittie (Snorf) Ford 15 Apr 1885; att Marion HS; att Cleveland, OH Commercial Coll; serv 12th Ind. Battery 1864-65; 1st tchr at White's Institute, Wabash Co.; admitted to Bar as an attorney 1882; f mbr Mississinewa MM; mbr M.E. Ch., Las Animas, CO; CW vet residing in Marion Soldier's Home when d 24 Jul 1898 (1,2,13,23,24,25,29,45,46,50,54,59,65,73)

BALDWIN, Asa T. - b Grant Co. 16 Mar 1835; s Thomas and Lydia (Thomas) Baldwin; 1st m Emily Kelly 11 Aug 1859; 2nd m Mrs. Mary E. (Jay) Overman 16 Mar 1885; att Earlham Coll; mbr Marion MM; d 13 Oct 1913 (1,7,10,16,23,24,25,29,31,32,41, 45,46,50,53,59,61,65)

BALDWIN, Daniel - b 4 Jun 1846; s Thomas and Lydia (Thomas) Baldwin; mbr Mississinewa MM; d 28 Dec 1852 (1,65)

BALDWIN, Emily (Kelly) - b Grant Co. 17 Mar 1836; dt Timothy and Avis (Sleeper) Kelly; m Asa T. Baldwin 11 Aug 1859; mbr Mississinewa MM; d 13 Mar 1884 (1,10,24,25,29,30 59,61,65)

BALDWIN, Harriet C. (Tharp) - b 14 Feb 1823; m Elias Baldwin 15 Oct 1840; d 11 Apr 1854 (10,29,59)

BALDWIN, Isabella (Lucas) - b IN 28 Oct 1837; dt Elijah and Matilda Lucas; m Terah Baldwin 4 Jan 1859; mbr Marion MM; d 19 Jan 1916 (1,10,24,29,37,43,46,50,53,58,59,64)

BALDWIN, Joseph W. - b Wayne Co. 13 Jan 1818; s Daniel and Christian (Wilcuts) Baldwin; 1833 came to Grant Co.; 16 Apr 1840 m Lydia Jane Stanfield; f mbr Mississinewa MM; d 20 Jun 1893 (1,10,11,21,22,23,24,25,29,45,46,47,50,54,57,65)

BALDWIN, Ket, Sr. - b IN 10 Sep 1859; s Terah and Isabella (Lucas) Baldwin; m Mary E. Evans ca 1882; mbr Marion MM; d 10 Mar 1912 (1,24,29,32,37,43,46,50,53,59,64,65)

BALDWIN, Ket, Jr. - b 11 Sep 1925; s Lucas and Marie (Fenstemaker) Baldwin; m Ruth; mbr Oak Ridge MM (1,29,46,59)

BALDWIN, Lydia (Thomas) - b Newgarden, Wayne Co. 25 Dec 1814; dt Stephen and Hannah (Mendenhall) Thomas; 26 Sep 1833 m Thomas Baldwin at Newgarden Friends MH; f mbr Deer Creek Anti-slavery MM; mbr Marion MM; d 21 May 1899 (1,8,13,17,21,23,24,25,28,29,43,45,46,47,49,50,55,59,65)

4 MISSISSINEWA FRIENDS CEMETERY

BALDWIN, Lydia Jane (Stanfield) - b TN 12 Nov 1823; dt David and Elizabeth (Beals) Stanfield; m Joseph W. Baldwin 16 Apr 1840; f mbr Back Creek MM; d 10 Oct 1892 (1,10,11,22, 23,29,41,46,47,50,53)

BALDWIN, Mary 'Polly' (Conner) - b SC 1807; dt Lewis and Margaret (McClaren) Conner; Wayne Co. 29 Jan 1820 m 1st Caleb Morris; 11 Aug 1867 m 2nd Edward Baldwin; d July 1877 (10,11,46,50,59)

BALDWIN, Mary (Rice) - b 1823; m Dillon Baldwin 11 Jul 1840; d 10 Jul 1853 (29,46)

BALDWIN, Mary E. (Jay) - b Dayton, OH 23 Sep 1842; dt Isaac and Rhoda (Cooper) Jay; 25 Feb 1863 m 1st Anderson O. Overman at Mississinewa Friends MH; 16 Mar 1885 m 2nd Asa T. Baldwin as his 2nd wife; mbr Marion MM; d ca 14 Dec 1924 (1,24,25,29,37,46,50,59,62,65,73)

BALDWIN, Mary E. 'Lizzy' (Evans) - b IN 8 Apr 1857; dt Eli K. and Charity (Jay) Evans; m Ket Baldwin, Sr. ca 1882; mbr Marion MM; d 31 Jan 1937 (1,29,37,46,50,53,59)

BALDWIN, Otto Kelly - b 20 Dec 1862; s Asa T. and Emily (Kelly) Baldwin; mbr Marion MM; d ca 26 May 1931 (1,7,24, 25,29,37,46,53,59,65)

BALDWIN, Ruth - prob b 9 Nov 1901; prob dt Elias and Flora E. (Bond) Baldwin; mbr Marion MM; 17 Nov 1927 (1,29)

BALDWIN, Sanford T. - b IN 2 Dec 1839; s Thomas and Mary (Davis) Baldwin; m Mary F. Howard; serv as 2nd Lieut., Co. H, 118th Ind. Inf.; f mbr Back Creek MM; d in Soldier's Home Hospital, Marion, IN 22 Jun 1919 (1,2,21,23,46,50,53,54,58)

BALDWIN, Terah - b Grant Co. 1 Feb 1837; s Thomas and Lydia (Thomas) Baldwin; m Isabella Lucas 4 Jan 1859; mbr Marion MM; d 19 Jul 1919 (1,10,23,24,25,29,37,41,43,45,46,50, 53,54,58,59,64,65)

BALDWIN, Thomas J. - b Richmond, Wayne Co. 26 Apr 1813; s Daniel and Christian (Willcuts) Baldwin; 26 Sep 1833 m Lydia Thomas at Newgarden Friends MH; f mbr Deer Creek Anti-slavery MM; mbr Marion MM; d 25 May 1899 (1,13,21,23,24,25,28,29,41,43,45,46,47,49,50,53,54,55,59,65)

BALLINGER, John - b Newberry Co., SC 31 Mar 1781; s James and Lydia (Taylor) Ballinger; m Sarah Small ca 1800; came to IN 1825; mbr White River MM; d 1827, 1st Quaker burial in this cem (1,8,17,23,25,27,46)

BALLINGER, Sarah (Small) - m John Ballinger ca 1800; mbr Mississinewa MM; d after Dec 1832 when aged/elderly (1,8, 25,29,46)

BANKS, Lacy/Lucy Ann (Weesner) - b ca 1840; 1st m Samuel Knight 27 Mar 1858; 2nd m Thomas H. Banks 5 Oct 1890; f mbr Marion MM; mbr M.E. Ch.; d 11 Aug 1921 at age 81 (1,7, 10,16,29,37,50)

BANKS, Thomas H. - b England 1840; m Lacy Ann (Weesner) Knight 5 Oct 1890; d 1 Nov 1902 (14,16,29,37,47)

BEARD, Ethel - dt Ezra Beard; b and d 26 Jun 1900 (29,37,47)

BEATTY, Mary A. - b 30 May 1817; m Samuel Beatty; d 28 Oct 1851 (29)

BEAUCHAMP, Curtis - b 21 Jul 1848; mbr W.M. Ch.; d 2 Jul 1866 (25,29)

BENBOW, Aaron - b Clinton Co., OH 5 Nov 1812; s John and Charity (Mendenhall) Benbow; 16 Nov 1836 m Catharine Elliott; f mbr Mississinewa MM; mbr W.M. Ch.; d 26 Oct 1875 (1,24,29,46,50,54,65)

BENBOW, Milly - b 13 Mar 1842; dt Aaron and Catharine (Elliott) Benbow; mbr Mississinewa MM; d 28 Jul 1843 (1,46,65)

BENNETT, Anna - m __; d 25 Jan 1899 at age 75 (13,37)

BESHORE, Martin V.D. - b 1 Jun 1842; s Peter and Mary (Whisler) Beshore; d 27 Aug 1859 (23,25,29,46)

BLOXHAM, Ephraim - b 13 Dec 1864; s James W. and Sarah J. (Lloyd) Bloxham; d 17 Jan 1866 (29)

BLOXHAM, Sarah J. (Lloyd) - b 3 Apr 1837; m James W. Bloxham 1 Sep 1863; d 13 Jan 1866 (10,29)

BOGUE, Gulielma 'Gula' (Thomas) - b 21 Nov 1807; dt Benjamin and Anna (Moorman) Thomas; 21 Dec 1826 m Jesse Bogue at New Garden Friends MH; mbr Mississinewa MM; d 15 Oct 1839 (1,8,46,55,59,65)

BOGUE, Leah - b 18 Feb 1832; dt Jesse and 'Gula' (Thomas) Bogue; mbr Mississinewa MM; d 29 May 1833 (1,29,46,59,65)

BOGUE, Martha (Carter) - b IN 9 Nov 1852; dt George and Mary (Buller) Carter; m Jesse Bogue as his 2nd wife; mbr Fairmount MM; d 31 Dec 1875 (1,25,29,46,50,59)

BOGUE, Milly (Baldwin) - b IN 1 Dec 1814; dt Daniel and Christian (Willcuts) Baldwin; 27 Nov 1834 m Barnaba Bogue; f mbr Deer Creek Anti-slavery MM; mbr Mississinewa MM; d 30 Oct 1882 (1,24,29,45,46,50,53,54,65)

BOND, Abigail (Hodgin) - b IN 22 Dec 1822; m Asa T. Bond as his first wife; mbr Oak Ridge MM; d 16 Apr 1881, may be bur in Back Creek Friends Cem (1,23,29,50,61)

BOND, Amos - b Wayne Co. 9 Apr 1814; s Joseph and Rachel (Harrold) Bond; 21 Nov 1839 m Lucy Coggeshall at New Garden Friends MH; 1865, Recorded Friends Minister; mbr Deer Creek MM; d 28 Feb 1896 (1,7,8,12,17,27,29,37,41,46,47,50, 53,54,64,65)

BOND, Anna E. (Wright) - b IN 14 Oct 1840; dt Joab and

Malinda (Elliott) Wright; 21 Feb 1864 m Joseph Bond; f mbr Mississinewa MM; d 8 Jan 1899 (1,10,13,29,33,37,46,47,50,65)

BOND, Anna (Smith) - dt Frank M. Smith; m Alva Bond; d ca 16 Nov 1908, funeral in Marion First Baptist Ch. (29,31,37)

BOND, Anna May - b 1864; d ca 12 Jul 1950 (29,37)

BOND, Asa T. - b IN 13 Nov 1829; s John H. and Emily (Hockett) Bond; 1st m Abigail Hodgin; 2nd m Mary 'Milly' (Coggeshall) Jay 4 Jul 1882; mbr Oak Ridge MM; d 29 Aug 1912 (1,16,29,32,37,50)

BOND, Edgar R. - b 23 Sep 1897; s Nathan Alva and Mary C. (Small) Bond; mbr Marion MM; d 17 Feb 1898 (1,29)

BOND, Edwin R. - b 23 Sep 1897; s Nathan Alva and Mary C. (Small) Bond; mbr Marion MM; d 3 Nov 1898 (1,29)

BOND, Enos L. - b Randolph Co. 14 Nov 1840; s Amos and Lucy (Coggeshall) Bond; 26 Nov 1865 m Mary Ann Carter; f Grant Co. Assessor; f mbr Mississinewa MM; mbr M.E. Ch.; d 28 Jan 1894 (1,10,11,25,29,46,50,53,54,61)

BOND, Everett A. - b 5 Jun 1890; s Nathan A. and Mary C. Bond; mbr Oak Ridge MM; d 5 Aug 1890 (1,29,47)

BOND, Hannah C. - b IN 24 Apr 1846; dt Amos and Lucy (Coggeshall) Bond; mbr Marion MM; d ca 8 Jul 1921 (1,29,37, 50,53,58,64,65)

BOND, Joseph - b Clinton Co., OH 13 May 1834; s Moses and Mary (Sears) Bond; 1st m Susannah Rich 14 Aug 1851; 2nd m Anne E. Wright 21 Feb 1864; during CW serv Co. F, 101st Ind. Inf.; d 15 Mar 1905 (10,19,29,37,46,50,54)

BOND, Lucy (Coggeshall) - b Surrey Co., NC 28 May 1816; dt Tristram and Elizabeth (Gardner) Coggeshall; 21 Nov 1839 m Amos Bond at New Garden Friends MH; mbr & Elder, Deer

Creek MM; d 30 Aug 1888 (1,12,29,46,50,61,64,65)

BOND, Mary - b 1908; dt Alva and Anna (Smith) Bond; d ca
23 Oct 1908 (29,31,37)

BOND, Mary - m Ocy Bond; d ca 29 Jul 1910 at age 78/88
(29,31,37)

BOND, Mary Ann (Carter) - b IN 1840; dt George and Mary
(Buller) Carter; 26 Nov 1865 m Enos L. Bond; d 25 Oct 1918
(1,10,11,25,29,50,53,58,59)

BOND, Mary C. (Small) - b Greensboro, Henry Co. 17 Nov
1863; dt Benjamin and Rachel Small; 19 Nov 1887 m Nathan
Alva Bond; mbr Marion MM; d 29 May 1898 (1,13,29)

BOND, Mary E. - d ca 25 Oct 1918 (29,37)

BOUSSAN, Alexander - b 1849; d 22 Apr 1885 (29)

BOWMAN, Isaac - b KY 7 Jul 1815; d 4 Apr 1871 (29,54)

BREEDLOVE, Asa - b VA 13 May 1830; d 18 Nov 1881 (7,29,
50,54)

BRITTAIN, James Harv - b 1850; m Mary J. Baldwin; d ca 16
Jul 1942 (7,11,29,37,59)

BRITTAIN, Mabel - b 6 Jun 1892; dt James Harv and Mary J.
(Baldwin) Brittain; d 8 Apr 1894 (29,47)

BRITTAIN, Mary J. (Baldwin) - b IN 1852; dt Henry J. 'Jack'
and Ruth (Tharp) Baldwin; m James Harv Brittain; d 16 Mar
1893 (11,29,50,59)

BRITTAIN, Thompson - b 1877; d ca 21 Jan 1959 (29,37)

BROCK, infant - child of E. B.; d ca 7 Sep 1895 (29,37)

BROOKS, Keziah C. (Gossett) - b 17 Mar 1848; dt George and Phebe Gossett; 16 Nov 1871 m William Brooks at Deer Creek Friends MH; mbr Mississinewa MM; d 13 May 1896 (1,12,29, 37,47,64)

BROOKS, William - b White Co. 5 Dec 1845; s Isaac and Priscilla Brooks; 16 Nov 1871 m Keziah C. Gossett at Deer Creek Friends MH; mbr Marion MM; d ca 28 Jun 1928 (1,7,29, 37,58,64)

BROWN, Hattie - wife of George Brown; mbr Marion MM; d ca 29 Jul 1899 at age 38, funeral in Marion Friends MH (1,13, 29,37,47)

BROWN, Thaddeus - b Henry Co. 31 Mar 1837; s Isaac and Mary Brown; Feb 1856 m Susanna Holden; f mbr Deer Creek MM; d after Apr 1889 (1,7)

BROWN, Walter - s M & M George Brown; d 15 Jul 1896 at age 2y (12,29)

BRUSS, Jima - d ca 13 Feb 1956 (37)

BRYAN, Grace (Yates) - dt William and Huldah (Thomas) Yates; 14 Jun 1896 m Earl Bryan; mbr Marion MM; d 25 Oct 1903 at age 27 (1,14,29,37,47)

BURNETT, David - d ca 17 Jul 1930 (29,37)

BURNETT, Grace V. (Humble) - b 1890; dt Ida Ballenger; 4 Aug 1922 m Fred L. Burnett; d 11 Jul 1930 at age 34 (29,35, 37,58)

BUTLER, Elizabeth (Morgan) - b 20 Oct 1828; dt Charles and Michel (Butler) Morgan; m Alfred Butler; mbr Mississinewa MM; d 2 Oct 1874 (1,7,9,29,61)

BUTLER, Jane (Symons) - b IN 16 Mar 1826; dt Nathan and Jane Symons; 22 Jul 1854 1st m Joseph Green (dec 1873); 17

Aug 1876 2nd m Alfred Butler (dec 1886); mbr Marion MM; d 17 Aug 1901 (1,10,14,29,37,47,50,53,59,65)

BYRD, William F. - b 9 Mar 1838; s A. and S.; d 14 Jul 1856 (29)

CABE, Thomas - b PA 8 Jun 1806; m Letitia Stratton; d 16 Nov 1887 (23,25,29,43,50,53,54)

CAMMACK, Bayard T. - b IN 30 Nov 1858; s Willis and Sarah (Jay) Cammack; 10 Mar 1882 m Martha J. 'Mattie' Osborn; mbr Marion MM; d 30 Aug 1892 (1,10,11,23,24,25,29, 41,47,50,59,61,73)

CAMMACK, Edgar J. - b 24 Aug 1877; s Willis and Sarah (Jay) Cammack; m Katherine Harris; student in a NY dental coll; mbr Oak Ridge MM; d 7 Feb 1905 (1,19,23,24,25,29,37,59)

CAMMACK, Elizabeth (Cornelius) - b 10 Aug 1849; dt George and Elizabeth (Eiler) Cornelius; 1st m Albert Cammack; 2nd m Willis Cammack 4 Jan 1883; mbr Oak Ridge MM; d Kokomo 22 Apr 1936 (1,29,37,39,53,59)

CAMMACK, Jane Emily (Haisley) - b 19 Jul 1839; dt John and Ann (Hawkins) Haisley; 25 Nov 1857 m Jesse Green Cammack; mbr Oak Ridge MM; d 8 Sep 1908 (1,8)

CAMMACK, Willis - b Bartholomew Co. 7 Oct 1833; s James and Penina (Cook) Cammack; 22 Aug 1855 at Centre Friends MH, Jonesboro, 1st m Sarah Jay (dec 1881); 2nd m Elizabeth (Cornelius) Cammack 4 Jan 1883; mbr Bethel MM; d 30 Jul 1906 (1,7,19,23,24,25,29,37,50,53,54,59,62)

CAMPBELL, __ - s Shesbadger B. and Emily (Jackson) Campbell; d 11 Oct 1854 (10,29)

CAMPBELL, Louisa - b 10 Sep 1842; dt Shesbadger B. and Emily (Jackson) Campbell; d 4 Jan 1848 (10,29)

CAMPBELL, Phebe E. - b 21 Jan 1847; dt S.C.? and L.? Campbell; d 5 Mar 1848? (29)

CAREY, Jane (Haisley) - b IN 19 Jul 1839; dt John and Ann (Hawkins) Haisley; at Oak Ridge Friends MH 25 Nov 1857 m Jesse G. Carey; mbr Oak Ridge MM; d 8 Sep 1908 (1,24,25,29, 31,46,50,59,62)

CAREY, Louise (Haines) - b 27 Dec 1876; dt Azariah and Mary E. Haines; m Charles Carey; mbr Marion MM; d 25 Feb 1909 (1,29,31,37,59)

CARL, Wayne - d ca 6 Jul 1895 (29,37)

CARTER, infant - child of Isaac Carter; d ca 7 Apr 1895 (29,37)

CARTER, Alice - b 30 Jun 1855; dt Isaac W. and Phebe (Whitson) Carter; mbr Oak Ridge MM; d 22 Dec 1861 (1,25,29,59)

CARTER, DeWitt - b Mill Twp. 29 Apr 1873; s William and Elizabeth (Knight) Carter; m Grace Lawson; grad Fairmount Friends Academy 1892; f mbr Deer Creek MM; mbr M.P. Ch., Jonesboro; d 19 Jan 1956 (1,25,29,37,44,59)

CARTER, Dwight M. - b 1895; s Henry D. and Sarah C. (Lamm) Carter; grad Marion Normal; d ca 22 Aug 1974 (25,29, 37,59)

CARTER, Elizabeth (Knight) - b IN 26 Aug 1851; dt Manoah and Martha 'Patsy' (Wilcuts) Knight; 9 Mar 1871 m William Carter; mbr South Marion MM; d 23 Apr 1928 (1,10,25,29,37, 50,58,59,64,65)

CARTER, Ethel Ann- b 14 Feb 1914; dt E.H. and L.A. Carter; d 26 Feb 1914 (29,37)

CARTER, George - b NC 12 Feb 1816; s Solomon and __ (Jane) Carter; 25 Nov 1836 m Mary Buller; mbr U.B. Ch.; d Mill Twp. 3 Apr 1889 (7,10,14,25,29,50,54,59,73)

CARTER, Grace (Lawson) - b 1877/78; m DeWitt Carter 27 Jan 1894; mbr Methodists; d ca 29 Apr 1947 (1,16,25,29,37,59)

CARTER, Harry - b 10 Jan 1894; s John A. and Minerva J. (Hiatt) Carter; mbr Oak Ridge MM; d 10 Feb 1894 (1,10,25,29, 46,59)

CARTER, Hazel May - b 15 Jan 1890; dt John A. and Minerva (Hiatt) Carter; mbr Marion MM; d ca 5 Jan 1965 (1,25,29,37, 46,59)

CARTER, Henry D. - b Mill Twp. 6 Sep 1852; s George and Mary (Buller) Carter; m Sarah C. Lamm 27 Mar 1880; d ca 15 Mar 1911, mbr Marion Christian Ch. (7,10,25,29,32,37,53,59)

CARTER, Isaac Wilson - b Clinton Co., OH 7 Feb 1835; s John and Hannah (Millikan) Carter; 19 Aug 1854 m Phebe Whitson at Back Creek Friends MH; 1855 came to Grant Co. from Clinton Co., OH; 1869 was Liberty Twp. Trustee; mbr Bethel MM; d 20 Nov 1907 (1,7,19,23,25,27,29,37,41,46,50,53,54,59,62)

CARTER, John Alpheus - b OH 27 Jan 1858; s Isaac W. and Phebe (Whitson) Carter; 26 Feb 1881 m Minerva J. Hiatt; mbr Marion MM; d ca 24 May 1942 (1,7,10,19,23,25,29,37,46,50, 53,59)

CARTER, Joseph Enos - b 4 Oct 1862; s Isaac W. and Phebe (Whitson) Carter; 19 Oct 1884 m Mary Della Coggeshall; mbr Oak Ridge MM; d 26 Jul 1945 (1,7,16,19,23,25,29,37,46,53,59)

CARTER, Mary (Buller) - b NC 14 Sep 1817; 25 Nov 1836 m George Carter; mbr U.B. Ch.; d 10 Apr 1903 (10,14,25,29,35,37, 47,50,59)

CARTER, Mary Della (Coggeshall) - b Grant Co. 31 May 1866; dt Eli and Anna (Bogue) Coggeshall; m Joseph E. Carter 19 Oct 1884; mbr Oak Ridge MM; d 16 Feb 1894 (1,11,29,46,59, 64,65)

CARTER, Mary L. - b 1892; dt Henry D. and Sarah C. (Lamm) Carter; grad, Marion Normal; d ca 30 Nov 1969 (10,25,29, 37,59)

CARTER, Minerva J. (Hiatt) - b Grant Co. 1860; dt Alfred and Lucinda (Thomas) Hiatt; 26 Feb 1881 m John A. Carter; mbr Oak Ridge MM; d ca 23 Aug 1938 (1,10,25,29,37,46,50,57,59)

CARTER, Omar Isaac - b Liberty Twp. 23 May 1882; s John A. and Minerva J. (Hiatt) Carter; f mbr Marion MM; d ca 9 Oct 1939 (1,25,29,37,46,57,59)

CARTER, Phebe (Whitson) - b Wayne Co. 5 Jun 1834; dt Amos and Rebecca (Peele) Whitson; 19 Aug 1854 m Isaac W. Carter at Back Creek Friends MH; mbr Oak Ridge MM; d 23 Mar 1898 (1,13,19,23,25,29,37,42,46,47,59,62)

CARTER, Rachel J. - b 20 Dec 1860; dt George and Mary (Buller) Carter; d 28 Sep 1862 (25,29,59)

CARTER, Rosetta - b 27 Sep 1865; dt Isaac W. and Phebe (Whitson) Carter; mbr Oak Ridge MM; d 5 Feb 1870, may be bur Deer Creek Friends Cem (1,29,46,59)

CARTER, Sarah C. (Lamm) - b Miami Co. 18 Jan 1857; dt Edmond and Johanna (Elliott) Lamm; 27 Mar 1880 m Henry D. Carter; mbr Friends; d ca 28 Feb 1946 (10,25,29,37,50,53,59)

CARTER, William - b IN 1850; s George and Mary (Buller) Carter; 9 Mar 1871 m Elizabeth Knight; mbr Back Creek MM; d 17 Feb 1912, funeral in Marion Friends MH (1,7,10,25,29,32, 50,59)

CARTER, William Albert - b Liberty Twp. 2 Jan 1860; s Isaac W. and Phebe (Whitson) Carter; 17 Mar 1885 m Anna May Jay; mbr Marion Friends; d 17 Feb 1910 (1,19,23,25,29,31,37,46, 53,59)

CHAMNESS, Rebecca J. (Lamb) - b Henry Co. 16 May 1836; dt

Miles and Nancy Lamb; 6 Mar 1855 m William S. Chamness; mbr Marion MM; d Indianapolis ca 28 Feb 1913 (1,7,29,32,33, 37,53)

CHAMNESS, William S. - b Randolph Co., NC 2 Nov 1824; s Nathan and Mary (McCracken) Chamness; 6 Mar 1855 m Rebecca J. Lamb; mbr Marion MM; d 18 Mar 1896 (1,12,17,29, 33,37,47,53)

CHAPPEL, Junie - d ca 7 Oct 1960 (29,37)

COATS, Milo W. - b 24 Jan 1876; d 19 Oct 1876 (29)

COGGESHALL, Anna (Bogue) - b IN 7 Oct 1840; dt Barnaba and Milly (Baldwin) Bogue; 31 Mar 1860 m Eli Coggeshall as his 1st wife; mbr & Overseer, Deer Creek MM; d 10 Jun 1880 (1,10,29,46,50,59,61,64,65)

COGGESHALL, Edna Grace - b 29 Nov 1883; dt Eli and Mary E. (Parker) Coggeshall; mbr Deer Creek MM; d 13 Aug 1898, funeral in Marion Friends MH (1,13,29,42,46,47)

COGGESHALL, Eli - b IN 20 Mar 1841; s Nathan and Guly (Shugart) Coggeshall; 1st m Anna Bogue 31 Mar 1860; 2nd m Mary E. Parker; mbr Marion MM; d 22 Mar 1916 (1,7,10,23,29, 37,41,46,50,53,54,58,59,64,65)

COGGESHALL, Ethel B. - b 11 Aug 1885; dt Eli and Mary E. (Parker) Coggeshall; mbr Deer Creek MM; d 13 Aug 1898, funeral in Marion Friends MH (1,13,29,42,46,47)

COGGESHALL, Jonathan - b NC 27 Oct 1802; s Peter and Pamela Coggeshall; m Abigail ca Oct 1835; mbr Back Creek MM; d 29 Dec 1871 (1,8,9,17,29,46,50,54,59,61)

COGGESHALL, Mary E. (Parker) - b IN 23 Sep 1850; prob dt Isaac and Malinda Parker; m Eli Coggeshall as his 2nd wife; mbr Marion MM; d 12 Mar 1923 (1,29,37,46,50,53,58)

COGGESHALL, Nathan - b NC 14 Feb 1813; s Tristram and Elizabeth (Gardner) Coggeshall; 1st m Guly Shugart 23 Aug 1831 at New Garden MH; 2nd m Martha E. Johnson; f mbr & Overseer Deer Creek Anti-slavery MM; mbr Marion MM; d 8 Apr 1902 (1,7,8,11,14,23,29,37,46,47,49,50,53,54,55,56,59,65)

COGGESHALL, Orange Barton - b 8 Jul 1873; s Eli and Anna (Bogue) Coggeshall; f mbr Deer Creek MM; d after Apr 1912 (1,7)

COLE, Alonzo S. - b 1884; m Maude Olga; d ca 2 Sep 1959 (29,37)

COLE, Maude Olga - b 1882; m Alonzo S. Cole; d ca 8 Mar 1942 (29,37)

COMER, John - b IN 3 Nov 1834; s William and Rebecca Comer; 6 Sep 1857 m Nancy Wilson; mbr Mississinewa MM; during CW serv Co. I and/or H, 101st Ind. Inf.; resident of Marion Soldier's Home; d 1 Apr 1908 (2,10,29,31,50)

CONNERS, Rhoda (Garner) - b SC 22 May 1816; dt Lelin and Ann Garner; 25 Aug 1850 m Tristram H. Conners (dec); mbr Oak Ridge MM; d 13 Dec 1904, funeral in Bethel Friends MH (1,10,14,23,29,37,50,53,59)

CONNERS, Tristram H. - b NC 31 Mar 1818; s Lewis and Margaret (McClaren) Conners; 25 Aug 1850 m Rhoda Garner; mbr W.M. Ch.; d 1 Dec 1887 (10,23,29,50,53,54,59)

COOK, Calvin Bond - b 14 Dec 1880; s Nathan W. and Rebecca A. (Miller) Cook; 5 Mar 1905 m Ida E. Moore; d 6 Jul 1908, funeral in Maple Run Friends MH (10,15,29,31,37,44, 46,56)

COOK, Emily Ann - b 25 May 1863; dt Joseph and Sarah (Purvis) Cook; mbr Mississinewa MM; d 11 Oct 1864 (1,62,65)

COOK, John W. - b 27 Nov 1862; s Jesse B. and Mary Cook;

mbr Mississinewa MM; d 20 Mar 1863 (1,65)

COOK, Nathan W. - b IN 10 Jul 1847; s William and Ruth (Small) Cook; 3 May 1874 m Rebecca A. Miller; mbr Deer Creek MM; d 4 1916 (1,7,10,14,23,29,37,46,50,58,59,64,65)

COOK, Rebecca Ann (Miller) - b 4 Apr 1853; dt Henry and Mary (Carrel) Miller; 3 May 1874 m Nathan W. Cook; mbr Deer Creek MM; d 16 Sep 1889 (1,10,29,46)

COOK, Sarah (Purvis) - b OH 1 Jul 1829; dt John and Mary (Patterson) Purvis; 25 Jan 1855 m Joseph Cook; mbr Deer Creek MM; d 1 Oct 1864 (1,29,46,50,62,64,65)

COOK, Sarah Ann - b IN 23 Aug 1827; dt William and Ruth (Small) Cook; mbr Deer Creek MM; d 6 Jul 1902 (1,23,29,37,46, 47,50,59,65)

COOK, William - b Guilford Co., NC 20 Jun 1803; s Joseph and Lydia (Wickersham) Cook; 16 Nov 1826 m Ruth Small; mbr Maple Run MM; d 31 Dec 1902 (14,23,25,29,37,46,47,50,54, 59,64,65)

COOPER, Elizabeth (Kennedy) - b 14 Sep 1782; dt John and Esther Kennedy/Canada; 1802 m Isaac Cooper in GA; mbr Mississinewa MM; d 3 Feb 1859 (1,18,29,30,53,60,62,65,71)

COUSINS, Michael - d ca 6 Aug 1941 (29,37)

COX, Alice - b 1875; dt Elias C. and Mary E. (Small) Cox; d 1 Sep 1897 (12,29,37,47)

COX, Elias Caswell - b 1854; s Henry and Julia Cox; 20 Jul 1873 m Mary Estella Small; d ca 12 Jan 1931 (10,29,37,46,58,59)

COX, Henry - b 4 Feb 1824; d 10 Feb 1884 (29)

COX, Julia E. (VanCannon) - b Randolph Co., NC 14 Dec 1829; sister of Ira VanCannon; d ca 22 Jan 1912 (7,29,32,37)

COX, Mary Estella (Small) - b IN 25 Feb 1854; dt Josiah and Nancy J. (Boxell) Small; 20 Jul 1873 m Elias Caswell Cox; f mbr Deer Creek MM; killed 22 Nov 1922 (1,10,29,37,46,50, 58,59)

COX, Mary R. (Knight) - b 20 Oct 1854; prob dt Sebborn Gonner and Mary E. (Parsons) Knight; 1st m Sylvanus Thomas 20 Sep 1873; 2nd m John W. Cox 8 Sep 1917; mbr Marion MM; d 22 May 1930 (1,10,29,35,37,58,58)

CRAMER, George - b Hamburg, Germany 2 Aug 1829; m Lucinda Bristendine; prob serv CW in Co. M, 5th Ind. Cav.; d 1887 (23,29,43)

CRAMER, Lucinda (Bristendine) - b 11 Jul 1831; m George Cramer; d 1888 (29,43)

CRAVENS, Emma (Small) - b IN 27 Nov 1859; dt Josiah and Nancy J. (Boxell) Small; 28 Jun 1883 m Albert M. Cravens; d 9 Mar 1894 (16,29,46,50,53)

CRAVENS, Luella - b 1870; d ca 27 Oct 1948 (29,37)

CROWELL, infant - dt Morton and Julia (Welch) Crowell; d ca 4 Nov 1909 (29,31,37,59)

CROWELL, infant - child of Morton and Julia (Welch) Crowell; d ca 19 Apr 1913 (29,37,59)

CROWELL, Benjamin - b Morris Co., NJ 1 Jan 1827; s Joseph and Margaret (White) Crowell; 1 Oct 1857 m Matilda R. Stevens; during CW serv Co. D, 153rd Ind. Inf.; mbr Marion MM; d 8 Feb 1898 (1,10,23,24,29,37,47,50,54,59,73)

CROWELL, Matilda R. (Stevens) - b Fairfield, OH 24 Mar 1836; dt Elias Robert and Matilda (Rose) Stevens; 1 Oct 1857 m Benjamin Crowell; mbr Marion MM; d 11 Jan 1914 (1,10, 23,24,29,37,50,58,59)

DAILY, Den(n)is - b 22 Oct 1791; m Mary 'Polly' H.; d 8 Apr 1861 (23,29)

DAILY, Mary 'Polly' H. - b VA 27 Oct 1807; m Denis Daily; d 19 Jul 1870 (29,54)

DAVIS, __ - wife of George Davis; d ca 4 Dec 1901 (29,37)

DAVIS, infant - child of George Davis; d ca 5 Dec 1901 (29,37)

DAVIS, infant - child of Oliver Davis; d ca 6 Dec 1901 (29,37)

DAVIS, Amos - b VA 30 Apr 1801; s Joseph Davis; m Mahala (Burson) Overman ca 1826; mbr Friends; d 16 Oct 1876 (25,29, 46,54)

DAVIS, Ann (Coggeshall) - b NC 5 Oct 1802; dt Tristram and Lucy Coggeshall; Wayne Co. 29 Jun 1826 m Wyllis Davis; mbr Deer Creek MM; d 11 Apr 1877 (1,8,29,46,50,61,64,65,72)

DAVIS, Bert - d ca 10 Feb 1956, bur in coffin with Nina L. Davis (29,37)

DAVIS, Charity Ann - b 7 Jul 1848; dt Jacob O. and Rebecca (Pearson) Davis; mbr Mississinewa MM; d 26 Dec 1850 (1,29,65)

DAVIS, Charlotte (Baldwin) - b Guilford Co., NC 11 May 1823; dt John and Charlotte (Payne) Baldwin; 15 Dec 1841 m George Davis; mbr Oak Ridge MM; d 8 Dec 1882, may be bur Oak Ridge Friends Cem (1,8,14,23,24,25,29,50,59)

DAVIS, Elwood - b IN 26 May 1835; s Wyllis and Ann (Coggeshall) Davis; 8 Dec 1855 m Rachel Shugart; Recorded Friends Minister; mbr Fairmount MM; d ca 24 Feb 1922 (1,7, 10,27,29,37,46,53,54,58,64,65)

DAVIS, Esther J. (Jones) - b 19 Mar 1823; dt Elisha and Rebecca (Pearson) Jones; 17 May 1866 m Jacob O. Davis as his

3rd wife; mbr Mississinewa MM; d 21 Aug 1867 (1,29,65)

DAVIS, Evangeline (Jay) - b IN 5 Jul 1854; dt Denny and Anna (Coggeshall) Jay; 14 Mar 1872 m Oliver Smith Davis; mbr Deer Creek MM; d Jan 1933 (1,10,23,24,25,29,40,46,50, 59,64)

DAVIS, George - b Montgomery Co., OH 12 May 1818; s Joseph and Catharine (Farmer) Davis; 15 Dec 1841 m Charlotte Baldwin; mbr Oak Ridge MM; d 23 Jul 1901, funeral in Bethel Friends MH (1,7,8,14,23,24,25,29,37,47,50,53,54,55,56,59)

DAVIS, Griffin - b 14 Mar 1844; s Wyllis and Ann (Coggeshall) Davis; mbr Mississinewa MM; d 18 Dec 1844 (1,29,46,65)

DAVIS, Harvey W. - b 12 Jul 1879; s Oliver S. and Evangeline (Jay) Davis; 13 Jul 1907 m Elizabeth Harmon; mbr Marion MM; d ca 6 Oct 1944 (1,15,23,24,29,37,59)

DAVIS, Jacob O. - b NC 1 Mar 1818; s Jesse and Alice Davis; 31 Oct 1838 m 1st Ann Bond in Wayne Co.; 12 May 1847 m 2nd Rebecca Pearson at Concord Friends MH, OH; 17 May 1866 m 3rd Esther Jones; 26 Jan 1870 m 4th Hannah Ratliff; mbr Mississinewa MM; d 3 Mar 1879 (1,7,29,30,46,50,54,59,61,65)

DAVIS, John W. - b 16 Oct 1822; d 28 Aug 1859 (29)

DAVIS, Joseph E. - b 9 Dec 1862; s George and Charlotte (Baldwin) Davis; 26 Mar 1885 m Nancy Ellen Doherty; mbr Oak Ridge MM; d 21 May 1930 (1,7,23,24,25,29,37,58,59)

DAVIS, Lorena A. (Lloyd) - b IN ca 1841; dt Thomas and Sarah J. Lloyd; m Nathan T. Davis 5 May 1861; d ca 22 Feb 1929 (10,29,37,50,53,58)

DAVIS, Mahala (Burson) - b VA 5 Apr 1793; m 1st Elisha Overman; m 2nd Amos Davis ca 1826; mbr Friends; d 13 Feb 1882 (25,29,46,53,54)

DAVIS, Margaret - b NC 23 Sep 1831; m Pritchard Davis; d 24 Aug 1888 (11,29,50,53)

DAVIS, Martha Ann - b IN 26 Oct 1852; dt Jacob O. and Rebecca (Pearson) Davis; mbr Mississinewa MM; d 4 Mar 1863 (1,50,62,65)

DAVIS, Mary A. - b IN 28 Nov 1853; dt Pritchard and Margaret Davis; d 15 Feb 1880 (29,50)

DAVIS, Mary Alice 'Allie' - b Grant Co. 7 Oct 1857; dt Jacob O. and Rebecca (Pearson) Davis; 1st grad, Marion High Sch; was a sch tchr; mbr Marion MM; d ca 19 May 1940 (1,29,37,50, 57,59,65)

DAVIS, Melissa - b IN 12 Feb 1850; dt George and Charlotte (Baldwin) Davis; mbr Oak Ridge MM; d 21 Aug 1861, may be bur Oak Ridge Friends Cem (1,23,24,29,50,59)

DAVIS, Melvin - b 29 Sep 1877; s Oliver S. and Evangeline (Jay) Davis; mbr Deer Creek MM; d 5 Aug 1880 (1,10,23,24,25, 29,59)

DAVIS, Nancy (Hiatt) - b 4 Apr 1817; dt William and Elizabeth (Sulgrove) Hiatt; 11 Mar 1835 m Jonathan B. Davis; d 15 Dec 1840 (10,25,29,46,59)

DAVIS, Nancy Ellen (Doherty) - b 21 Feb 1864; dt Elam and Nancy (Wilson) Doherty; 26 Mar 1885 m Joseph E. Davis; mbr Oak Ridge MM; d 8 Apr 1901, funeral in Bethel Friends MH (1,14,24,29,37,46,59)

DAVIS, Nathan T. - b IN 12 Nov 1838; m Lorena A. Lloyd 5 May 1861; pastor, Roseburg U.B. Ch.; d 23 Jun 1897 (10,12,29, 37,53,54)

DAVIS, Nina L. - d ca 10 Feb 1956, bur in coffin with Bert Davis (29,37)

DAVIS, Oliver Smith - b Liberty Twp. 9 Nov 1851; s George and Charlotte (Baldwin) Davis; 14 Mar 1872 m Evangeline Jay; mbr Marion MM; d ca 24 Jun 1927 (1,7,10,23,24,25,29,37, 46,50,53,59,64)

DAVIS, Pritchard - b IN 26 Apr 1827; m Margaret; d 10 Jan 1892 (29,47,50,53)

DAVIS, Rachel - (29)

DAVIS, Rachel (Shugart) - b IN 4 Nov 1838; dt Henry and Susanna Shugart; 8 Dec 1855 m Rev. Elwood Davis; mbr Friends; d 24 Jan 1910, funeral in Marion Friends MH (1,10, 29,31,37,50,64,65)

DAVIS, Rebecca (Pearson) - b OH 6 Sep 1819; dt Robert and Catherine (Price) Pearson; 12 May 1847 at Concord Friends MH, OH m Jacob O. Davis as his 2nd wife; mbr Mississinewa MM; d 25 Oct 1861 (1,29,30,46,50,60,62,65)

DAVIS, Rosamond - b Mill Twp. 12 Jan 1860; dt Elwood and Rachel (Shugart) Davis; mbr Mississinewa MM; d 12 Dec 1875 (1,29,50,64,65)

DAVIS, Susan H. - b IN 20 May 1854; dt Jacob O. and Rebecca (Pearson) Davis; mbr Mississinewa MM; d 17 Jan 1873 (1,29, 50,57,61,65)

DAVIS, Thomas Ellwood - b IN 17 May 1859; s Jacob O. and Rebecca (Pearson) Davis; mbr Mississinewa MM; d 4 May 1862 (1,29,50,60,62,65)

DAVIS, William S. - b Wilmington, OH 12 Mar 1839; s Hiram and Mary Davis; 21 Aug 1865 m Berthenia Painter; mbr Deer Creek MM; d Jonesboro 1 Mar 1930 (1,2,29,58,59)

DAVIS, Wilson H. - b IN 25 Nov 1843; s Jacob O. and Ann (Bond) Davis; mbr Marion MM; was a Medical Dr.; d ca 20 May 1908 (1,29,37,50,57,59,65)

DAVIS, Wyllis - b NC 19 Jul 1800; Wayne Co. 29 Jun 1826 m Ann Coggeshall; early tchr in Mississinewa Friends Sch; mbr Deer Creek MM; d 22 Jun 1883 (1,7,8,25,29,46,50,53,54,64,65,72)

DEVELBISS, Nancy Monciean? (Sanders) - 22 Dec 1889 m Luther Develbiss; d ca 21 Jan 1899 (13,16,29,37)

DRAPER, Calvin W. - b IN 1840; s Joshua and Huldah (Pearson) Draper; 23 Feb 1860 m Charlotte Modlin; f mbr Marion MM; d ca 13 Feb 1920 (1,10,29,37,46,50,54,59,72)

DRAPER, Cassie - b 1851; d ca 1 Oct 1928 (29,37)

DRAPER, Gerald - b IN 26 Nov 1834; 25 Mar 1858 m Susan Nelson; d 9 Aug 1863 (10,29,46,50)

DRAPER, Huldah (Pearson) - b Surry Co., NC 16 Mar 1809; dt Nathan and Huldah (Pearson) Pearson; Wayne Co. 5 May 1825 m Joshua Draper; mbr Marion MM; d 8 Oct 1888 (1,17,29, 33,46,50,59,72)

DRAPER, John - b NC 1 Jul 1803; prob s Josiah and Merium Draper; prior to 16 Nov 1822 m Margaret; d 26 Dec 1866 (9,17, 29,30,50,53,59)

DRAPER, Joshua - b NC 13 Oct 1802; s Josiah and Merium Draper; Wayne Co. 5 May 1825 m Huldah Pearson; f mbr Duck Creek MM; d 7 Jun 1876 (7,17,29,30,33,46,50,54,59,72)

DRAPER, Noah - b IN 28 Sep 1837; s John and Margaret Draper; 11 Jun 1853 m Sarah E. Douglass; 2nd m 26 Feb 1857 Jane Hiatt; d 20 May 1893 (10,29,46,50,53,59)

DRAPER, Sarah E. (Douglass) - b 25 Oct 1833; 11 Jun 1853 m Noah Draper; d 6 May 1855 (10,29,46,59)

DRUCKEMILLER, Asbury - b 17 Feb 1853; s John and Catherine Druckemiller; d 9 Mar 1854 (29)

DRUCKEMILLER, Harriet - b 30 Nov 1855; dt John and Catherine Druckemiller; d 23 Nov 1871 (29)

DRUCKEMILLER, Melvin - b 20 Dec 1859; s John and Catherine Druckemiller; d 21 May 1861 (29)

DRULEY, Emma - b 20 Dec 1867; dt William J. and Louisa (Romine) Druley; d 3 Oct 1869 (10,29)

DRYSDALE, Mary - b Sep 1871; dt J.R. and C. Drysdale; d 28 Oct 1873 (29)

EAKINS, Elizabeth - b 1840; d 1873 (29)

EATON, Bertha M. (Cloud) - b 1890; 28 Aug 1909 m Burr S. Eaton; d ca 2 Jan 1970 (15,29,37)

EATON, Blanche - d Apr 1895 (29,37)

EATON, Burr S. - b 30 Nov 1884; s Radamanthus M. and Mary C. (Gibson) Eaton; 28 Aug 1909 m Bertha M. Cloud; f mbr Back Creek MM; d ca 1 Aug 1972 (1,15,29,37)

EATON, Mary C. (Gibson) - b 23 May 1860; dt John and Ruth (Watkins) Gibson; 30 Jan 1884 m Radamanthus C. Eaton; mbr Back Creek MM; d 1929 (1,16,29,42)

EATON, Radamanthus M. - b GA 7 Apr 1851; s Jackson H. and Martha E. (McWilliams) Eaton; 30 Jan 1884 m Mary C. Gibson; mbr Back Creek MM; d 21 Jul 1924 (1,7,16,29,37,58)

EATON, Virginia - dt Burr S. and Bertha M. (Cloud) Eaton; mbr Back Creek MM; d ca 14 Aug 1910 (1,29,37)

EDGERTON, Jesse - b Miami Co. 12 Jun 1858; s Calvin and Hannah Edgerton; m Sarah A. Shugart 10 Oct 1878; mbr & Overseer, Deer Creek MM; d 8 Nov 1897, funeral in Marion Friends MH (1,7,10,12,25,29,47,50,59)

EDGERTON, Sarah Ann 'Sallie' (Shugart) - b 20 Aug 1857; dt
John and Rebecca (Guyer) Shugart; m Jesse Edgerton 10 Oct
1878; mbr Oak Ridge MM; d ca 26 Jul 1934 (1,10,12,25,29,46,59,
64,65)

EDMINSTON/EDMONDSON, Glena C. - b 1891; dt Rhoda;
step-dt Grant Stallings; d 8 Oct 1896 (12,16,29)

ELDRIDGE, Daniel C. - b NY 23 Nov 1826; m Susan M.; mbr
Methodist Ch.; d 24 Apr 1901 (14,29,37,47)

ELDRIDGE, Susan M. - b 5 Jun 1835; m Daniel C. Eldridge; d
30 Nov 1900 (13,29,37)

ELLIOTT, twin infants - b & d 20 Oct 1873; children of Isaac
and Mary R. (Small) Elliott (29,46)

ELLIOTT, Bethuel - b 25 Jul 1836; child of Isaac and Rachel
(Overman) Elliott; mbr Mississinewa MM; d 31 Mar 1847
(1,46,65)

ELLIOTT, Hannah (Morris) - b 19 Sep 1827; dt Aaron and
Nancy (Thomas) Morris; m Exum Elliott 22 Jan 1851; mbr
Mississinewa MM; d 11 Aug 1851 (1,25,29,51,59,65)

ELLIOTT, Isaac - b 16 Mar 1801 Randolph Co., NC; s Exum
and Catherine (Lamb) Elliott; 13 Dec 1818 m Rachel Overman; mbr Mississinewa MM; d 2 Apr 1871 (1,21,25,25,29,46,
50,59,65)

ELLIOTT, Isaac - b IN 6 Jul 1859; s Ephraim and Eunice (Pemberton) Elliott; mbr Mississinewa MM; d 22 Sep 1860 (1,29,46,
50,65)

ELLIOTT, Jemima - b 22 Sep 1828; m J.W. Elliott; d 26 Jan
1851 (29)

ELLIOTT, Mary Elizabeth - b 19 Sep 1866; dt William S. and
Ruth (Wilson) Elliott; mbr Fairmount MM; d 21 Sep 1866

(1,25,29,46)

ELLIOTT, Rachel (Overman) - b 19 Sep 1800 Grayson Co., VA; dt Ephraim and Rachel (Small) Overman; 13 Dec 1818 m Isaac Elliott; 1822 came to Grant Co.; mbr & Elder, Mississinewa MM; d 5 Apr 1873 (1,21,24,25,25,29,46,50,59,61,65)

FADLEY, George - d Sep 18__ (29)

FAULKNER, Maude - b 3 Mar 1878; m Edward Faulkner; d Liberty Twp. 16 Nov 1924 (29,37,58)

FEAR, Iva/Ida L. - b 1876; d ca 28 May 1956 (29,37)

FELTON, Arsula 'Lula' (Cammack) - 15 Aug 1874; dt Albert and Elizabeth (Cornelius) Cammack; 25 Mar 1892 m Robert Edward Felton; mbr Oak Ridge MM; d 17 Aug 1903, funeral in Marion Friends MH (1,14,16,25,29,37,47,53,59)

FISHER, John - b IN 1821; d 1892 (29,50)

FOWLER, Frances - b 24 Jul 1818; m Powell H. Fowler; d 12 Oct 1854 (25,27,29)

FOWLER, George - b 4 Nov 1844; d 12 Nov 1854 (29)

FOWLER, Louise May Belle 'Lida' - b 5 Jul 1862; mbr Fairfield Chapel M.E. Ch.; d 2 Nov 1881 (11,29)

FOWLER, Lutilia - b 4 May 1851; d 13 Dec 1854 (29)

FOWLER, Mary E. - b 9 Apr 1853; dt Powell H. and Frances Fowler; d 12 Oct 1854 (25,29)

FOWLER, Sarah L. - b IN 16 Aug 1827; d 27 Nov 1883 (29,50)

FRAME, Colene - b 1895; d Dec 1913 (29)

FRAME, Edna (Carter) - 1 Mar 1923 m Walter Frame; d

Jonesboro 24 Dec 1923 (35,37,58)

GARDNER, Calvin - s Libni and Ann (Starbuck) Gardner; Henry Co. 27 Oct 1838 m Hannah Chew; mbr Oak Ridge MM; d 12 Sep 1899 at age 85y, 1m, 10da (1,13,29,37,70)

GARDNER, Edward S. - b NC ca 1827; m Nancy; mbr Marion MM; killed in RR accident Dec 1892 (1,7,11,50)

GARDNER, Nancy - b NC; m Edward S. Gardner (dec); mbr Marion MM; d 25 Jan 1896 at age 66 (1,12,29,37,50)

GARNER, twin infants - s & dt Cyrus M. and Josephine E. (Shugart) Garner; both d 2 Apr 1884 (29)

GARNER, Josephine E. (Shugart) - b 29 Dec 1863; dt Isaiah R. and Ann (Whitson) Shugart; 7 Apr 1883 m Cyrus M. Garner; mbr Oak Ridge MM; d 4 Jul 1884 (1,11,16,29,46)

GAUNTT, Stella J. - dt H. and M. Gauntt; d 17 Feb 18__ (29)

GIBSON, Martha J. 'Mattie' (Osborn) - b 24 Oct 1851; dt Adam and Paulina (Clark) Osborn; 10 Mar 1882 m Bayard T. Cammack; m 2nd Daniel F. Gibson 30 Nov 1899; Recorded Friends Minister, 1895; mbr Marion MM; d ca 16 Apr 1923 (1,7,10,15,24,29,37,42,59)

GIBSON, Rosa - d ca 3 Apr 1896 (29,37)

GOLDSMITH, Bayard C. - b 1920; d 5 Mar 1940 (29,37)

GOLDSMITH, Mary Lee (Cammack) - b 27 Aug 1889; dt Baird and Martha (Osborn) Cammack; 20 Dec 1911 m Fred C. Goldsmith; mbr Back Creek MM; d 20 Oct 1954 (1,29,35,37,42)

GOODRICK, Andrew H. - b Clinton Co., OH 8 May 1840; 29 Aug 1865 m Rachel Leverton; 2nd m Lucy Jones 5 Sep 1905; during CW serv Co. C, 12th Ind. Inf.; mbr Deer Creek MM; d 9 Jan 1917 (1,2,10,15,29,50,53,54,58)

GOODWIN, Ella - b Georgetown, Harrison Co., OH 1 Sep 1869; dt Jesse and Alice A. Goodwin; mbr Oak Ridge MM; d 2 Dec 1886 (1,11)

GOODWIN, Mary Ida - b 16 Apr 1867; dt Jesse and Alice A. Goodwin; mbr Oak Ridge MM; d 12 May 1887 (1,29)

GORDON, Susanna (Hiatt) - b NC 18 Oct 1797; m Richard Gordon; mbr Back Creek MM; d 2 Apr 1869 (1,23,24,50)

GOTSCHALL, infant - d 29 Apr 1867 (29)

GOTSCHALL, Boney - s Benjamin R. and Sarah J. Gotschall; d 28 Sep 1874 (29)

GOTSCHALL/GUTSHELL, Clark - b 1849; m Mary; d ca 5 May 1895 (29,37)

GOTSCHALL, Mary - b 1861; m Clark Gotschall; d 29 Sep 1898 (13,29,47)

GOTSCHALL, Sarah - m Benjamin A. Gotschall; d 14 Jul 1896, funeral in M.E. Ch. (12,29,37,53)

GOUGH, Georgia - d ca 11 Feb 1973 (29,37)

GREEN, Arminnie - dt C.W. and H.J. Green (29)

GREEN, Drusilla Ann - b 28 Jul 1857; dt Joseph and Jane (Symons) Green; mbr Mississinewa MM; d 15 Oct 1860 (1,29 59,65)

GREEN, Durbin Ward - b 8 Oct 1861; s Joseph and Jane (Symons) Green; m Alice Abbott 9 Dec 1886; mbr Mississinewa MM; d 18 Jan 1888 (1,11,16,65)

GREEN, Joseph - b Ireland 25 Dec 1807; 22 Jul 1854 m Jane Symons as his 2nd wife; mbr Mississinewa MM; d 3 Jan 1873 (1,10,14,29,54,59,65)

GREEN, Joseph - mbr Mississinewa MM; d 5 Jan 1876 (29,65)

GREEN, Lydia Jane - b IN 6 Aug 1856; dt Joseph and Jane (Symons) Green; mbr Mississinewa MM; d 18 Nov 1873 (1,11,29, 50,65)

GREEN, Nathan - b 6 Aug 1856; s Joseph and Jane (Symons) Green; mbr Mississinewa MM; d 13 Aug 1856 (1,29,65)

GREEN, Rachel Ellen (Penrod) - b IN 1846; 22 Apr 1867 m William L. Green; f mbr Marion MM; d 30 Nov 1924 (1,10,29, 37,50,58,59)

GREEN, William L. - b IN 1845; s Joseph Green; step-son of Jane (Symons) Butler; 22 Apr 1867 m Rachel Ellen Penrod; during CW serv Co. E, 33rd Iowa Inf.; mbr Marion MM; d 22 Nov 1920 (1,7,10,29,37,50,53,58,59)

GUTSHALL, Catherine - b IN 1825; m Moses Gutshall; d 24 Aug 1902 (14,29,37,47,54)

GUTSHALL, Lesley - b 10 Nov 1858; s Peter and C. 'Polly' (Druckemiller) Gutshall; d 30 May 1860 (10,29,59)

GUTSHALL, Moses - b 1820; m Catherine; d 1870 (29)

GUYER, infant - child of Henry Guyer; d 28 Sep 1902 at age 4m (14,29,37,47)

HAINES/HANES, Azariah - b Grant Co. 30 Sep 1856; s Azariah and Elizabeth (Pierce) Haines; 10 Aug 1876 m Mary E. Cabe; f mbr Marion MM; d ca 5 Feb 1942 (1,7,10,23,29,37,59)

HAINES, Mary E. 'Mollie' (Cabe) - b IN 7 Jul 1859; dt Thomas and Letitia (Stratton) Cabe; 10 Aug 1876 m Azariah Haines; mbr Marion MM; d 21 Jan 1901, funeral in Marion Friends MH (1,10,14,29,37,47,50,56,59)

HAISLEY, Anna (Hawkins) - b Wayne Co. 8 Dec 1817; dt

Henry and Ann Hawkins; m John Haisley 13 May 1838 at Dover Friends MH; mbr Oak Ridge MM; d 27 Dec 1896, funeral in Oak Ridge Friends MH (1,8,12,24,25,29,37,46,47, 50,59)

HAISLEY, John - b NC 7 Nov 1817; s Jesse and Ruth Haisley; 13 May 1838 m Anna Hawkins at Dover Friends MH; mbr Mississinewa MM; d 6 Nov 1879, may be bur Oak Ridge Friends Cem (1,7,8,12,24,25,29,46,50,59)

HAM, James W. - s Edward and A. Ham; d ca 13 Jan 1907 at age 2y (19,29,37)

HAMMOND, Joseph - b 6 Sep 1843; m Hannah; mbr Marion MM; d 24 May 1904 (1,7,14,29,33,37)

HANN, John - b 18 Nov 1843; prob s Benjamin and Mary Ann Hann; killed on railroad 19 Nov 1868 (27,29,50)

HARDIN, Catherine (Forbes) - b Guilford Co., NC 24 Mar 1825; m John Hardin 2 Jun 1846; d 24 Oct 1892, funeral in 2nd Friends MH, Marion (11,29)

HARDIN, John - b Crawford Co., OH 20 Apr 1818; s John and Hannah Hardin; m 1st Catherine Forbes 2 Jun 1846; m 2nd; mbr Marion MM; d 18 Jun 1907, funeral in Marion Friends MH (1,19,29,37)

HARMON, Glyde - dt M & M Frank F. Harmon; d 25 Apr 1903 at age 7y (14,29,37,47)

HARRIS, David Elmer - b 22 Dec 1871; s David S. and Rachel (Wiant) Harris; 3 Oct 1892 m Minnie Bell Cox; mbr Deer Creek MM; d ca 30 Oct 1957 (1,16,24,25,29,37,59,64)

HARRIS, David S. - b Franklin Twp. 22 Nov 1838; s Thomas and Mary (Shugart) Harris; 15 Dec 1861 m Rachel Wiant; Recorded Friends Minister; mbr Deer Creek MM; d 12 Sep 1924 (1,10,24,25,29,37,42,44,50,54,58,59,64,65)

HARRIS, Edward D. - b 28 Aug 1887; s Elam H. and Clara (McNair) Harris; mbr Deer Creek MM; d 28 Aug 1887 (1,25,29)

HARRIS, Elam H. - b Grant Co. 28 Jun 1864; s David S. and Rachel (Wiant) Harris; 13 Nov 1886 m Clara McNair; mbr Deer Creek MM; d 17 Nov 1913 (1,16,24,25,29,32,37,59,64)

HARRIS, Minnie Bell (Cox) - b Oct 1874; dt William Penn and Flora E. Cox; m David E. Harris 3 Oct 1892; mbr Marion MM; d ca 5 Sep 1937 (1,16,24,25,29,37,59)

HARRIS, Rachel (Wiant) - b Carroll Co., OH 29 Sep 1838; dt Harrison and Rachel (Betty) Wiant; 15 Dec 1861 m David S. Harris; mbr Deer Creek MM; d 6 Mar 1910, funeral in Deer Creek Friends MH (1,10,24,25,29,31,37,59,64)

HAWKINS, infant - s Josiah R. and Emma (Chaney) Hawkins; mbr Marion MM; d ca 18 Feb 1897 at age 20m, funeral in Marion Friends MH (1,12,29,37)

HAYNES, Rhoda J. - b 30 Aug 1857; m S.S. Haynes; d 14 Dec 1878 (29)

HELM, Benjamin F. - b OH 1847; 18 Sep 1873 m Millicent Coggshall; d Aug 1924 (10,29,50,54,59)

HELM, Martha Teal - b 6 Apr 1873; d 14 Dec 1951 (29,37)

HELM, Millicent (Coggeshall) - b IN 20 Mar 1852; dt Nathan and Guly (Shugart) Coggeshall; 18 Sep 1873 m Benjamin F. Helm; f mbr Mississinewa MM; mbr M.E. Ch.; d ca 23 Nov 1934 (1,10,29,37,46,50,53,59,65)

HELM, Nancy Jane (Ellis) - b OH 14 Aug 1839; dt Robert and Anna Ellis; 1st m Walter D. Jay 17 Oct 1857; 2nd m Francis M. Helm 11 Oct 1873; f mbr Mississinewa MM; mbr Marion M.E. Ch.; d 27 Aug 1920 (1,10,29,37,42,46,50,65,73)

HELM, Verling W. - b 19 Mar 1875 (29)

HELM, Verling - d ca 13 Sep 1967 (29,37)

HENRY, Katie - b 1863; m; d 21 Feb 1914 at age 53 (29,37,58)

HIATT, Clifford - b Jan 1902; d ca 3 Nov 1903 (29,37)

HIATT, Eliza Ann (Lacey) - b IN 1856; dt James and Elizabeth Lacey; 28 Dec 1876 m George W. Hiatt; mbr Deer Creek MM; d ca 17 Jun 1928 (1,10,29,37,50,58,59)

HIATT, Elizabeth (Sulgrove) - b 1773; m William Hiatt 5 Feb 1799; prob mbr Mississinewa MM; d 26 May 1849 (1,29,46,59)

HIATT, George W. - b Grant Co. 6 Mar 1854; s Alfred and Lucinda (Thomas) Hiatt; 28 Dec 1876 m Eliza Ann Lacey; mbr South Marion MM; d 6 Sep 1923 (1,10,29,37,50,58,59)

HIATT, Gracy - b 26 Mar 1880; dt George W. and Eliza A. (Lacey) Hiatt; mbr Deer Creek MM; d 5 Oct 1881 (1,29,59)

HIATT, Joseph - b OH 1807; s William and Elizabeth (Sulgrove) Hiatt; Delaware Co. m Sarah Ballinger 20 Nov 1826 (25,29,46,59)

HIATT, Margaret 'Peggy' (Sullivan) - b Guilford Co., NC 15 Oct 1812; 1832 m Lemuel Hiatt; mbr Mississinewa MM; d 14 May 1896 (1,12,50)

HIATT, Meredith - s A.L. and R. Hiatt; d Aug 1898 at age ca 29y (13,29)

HIATT, Rebecca - m R.L. Hiatt?; d Ocean Peake, CA ca 4 Oct 1911 (29,32,37)

HIATT, William - b Guilford Co., NC 18 Aug 1775; s Isaac and Martha (Thomas) Hiatt; m Elizabeth Sulgrove 5 Feb 1799 in Guilford Co., NC; dismissed by Mississinewa MM; d 4 Mar 1855 (1,29,46,59)

HILL, Amanda - b 1853; m James Monroe Hill; d Delphos, OH ca 19 Jan 1910 (29,31,37)

HILL, James Monroe - b IN 1850; m Amanda; d Des Moines, IA Apr 1894 (11,29,54)

HILL, Maude - b 1879; d ca 3 Jan 1905 (19,29,37)

HILLERY, Alvina (Hockett) - b 6 Sep 1871; dt Benjamin A. and Cynthia (Edgerton) Hockett; 1st m Eli R. Thomas ca 1887; 2nd m __ Hillery after 1904; mbr Amboy MM; d 22 Mar 1930 (1,29,37,58)

HINKLE, Dillard D. - b 17 May 1946; d 26 May 1982 (29)

HOCKETT, Eli - b IN 10 Nov 1836; s Phillip and Mirium (Bundy) Hockett; at Mississinewa Friends MH 23 Sep 1857 m Hannah Marie Cook; 2nd m Hannah McIntire 27 Jun 1885; during CW serv Co. I, 101st Ind. Inf.; mbr Marion MM; d 9 Aug 1916 (1,2,16,29,44,46,50,54,58,65)

HOLLINGSWORTH, Aaron - b 9 Mar 1837; s Isaac and Jane (Coppock) Hollingsworth; mbr Mississinewa MM; d of typhoid fever 19 Mar 1859 (1,29,46,60,62,65)

HOLLINGSWORTH, Eli - b Darke Co., OH 13 Nov 1822; s Isaac and Jane (Coppock) Hollingsworth; 1st m Huldah Jones 25 Jun 1845; 2nd m Mary (Pearson) Malott; m 3rd Mary Jane Peebles 22 Feb 1894; mbr Marion MM; d 16 Jan 1907, funeral in Marion Friends MH (1,7,19,16,24,29,37,46,50,59,65,73)

HOLLINGSWORTH, Frank - b 19 Sep 1874; s I.L. and E.T.; d 23 Dec 1874 (29)

HOLLINGSWORTH, Huldah (Jones) - b OH 1 Nov 1826; dt Richard and Hannah (Thomas) Jones; 25 Jun 1845 m Eli Hollingsworth; mbr & Elder, Mississinewa MM; d 2 Mar 1887 (1,24,29,46,50,59,61,65)

HOLLINGSWORTH, Isaac, Sr. - b NC 6 Apr 1795; s Henry and Sarah Hollingsworth; 1st m Jane Coppock 6 Nov 1816 in Union Friends MH, Miami Co., OH; 2nd m Anna (Hutchins) Jones 13 Dec 1860 at Wabash Friends MH; mbr Mississinewa MM; d 18 Jul 1874 (1,7,24,29,30,46,50,53,54,59,62,65)

HOLLINGSWORTH, Isaac, Jr. - b IN 19 Aug 1841; s Isaac and Jane (Coppock) Hollingsworth; m Emily Thomas 26 Feb 1863; mbr Mississinewa MM; d 30 Mar 1882 (1,10,11,29,50,53,54,65)

HOLLINGSWORTH, Jane (Coppock) - b 28 Feb 1801; dt John and Mary Ann Coppock; m Isaac Hollingsworth, Sr. 6 Nov 1816 in Union Friends MH, Miami Co., OH; mbr Mississinewa MM; d of typhoid fever 16 Apr 1859 (1,24,29,30,46,59,60, 62,65)

HOLLINGSWORTH, Jane J. - b 14 Jul 1843; dt Isaac and Jane (Coppock) Hollingsworth; mbr Mississinewa MM; d 17 Jan 1859 (1,29)

HOLLINGSWORTH, John - b 14 Jan 1818; s Isaac and Jane (Coppock) Hollingsworth; 23 Oct 1839 m Lydia Jones; mbr Mississinewa MM; d 22 Feb 1843 (1,29,46,52,65)

HOLLINGSWORTH, John F. - b Wabash Co. 28 Aug 1866; s Eli and Huldah (Jones) Hollingsworth; mbr Deer Creek MM; d 4 Dec 1890 (1,29,46,59)

HOLLINGSWORTH, Julia Ann - b 13 Mar 1833; dt Isaac and Jane (Coppock) Hollingsworth; mbr Mississinewa MM; d of typhoid fever 30 Apr 1859 (1,29,46,60,62)

HOLLINGSWORTH, Matilda - b IN 20 Apr 1854; dt Eli and Huldah (Jones) Hollingsworth; mbr Mississinewa MM; d 12 Mar 1872 (1,29,46,50,59)

HOLLINGSWORTH, Nathan - b SC 27 Mar 1769; mbr Mississinewa MM; d 12 Aug 1847 (1,17,29,65)

HOLLINGSWORTH, Walter - (29)

HOLLINGSWORTH, Wright - b 12 Feb 1835; s Isaac and Jane
(Coppock) Hollingsworth; m Margaret Stanley 2 Oct 1858;
mbr Mississinewa MM; d near Xenia of typhoid fever 24 Mar
1859 (1,18,29,46,60,62,65,71)

HOLMAN/HOLMES, Elizabeth (Love) - b PA ca 1820; m
William Homes/Holmes 8 Dec 1842; d Apr 1896 at age 76
(10,11,29,37)

HOLMAN, Jessie L. (Pemberton) - b 1897; m Phillip Holman
19 Jul 1916; d 1993 (29,35)

HOMES, James L. - b IN 30 Jul 1851; s William and Elizabeth
(Love) Homes/Holmes; d 3 Jan 1877 (29,50)

HOMES/HOLMES, William - b OH 22 Jul 1819; 8 Dec 1842 m
Elizabeth Love; d 3 Feb 1871 (10,29,50,54)

HOWELL, Charles J. - b IN 2 Aug 1845; s Jeremiah and Sarah
J. (Jessup) Howell; 6 Jan 1866 m Sarah Ellen Carey; serv in
CW in Co. F, 34th Ind. Inf. and in Fairmount Militia Co.
(Home Guards); mbr Oak Ridge MM; d 2 Sep 1911 (1,2,10,22,
23,29,32,44,50,54,59)

HUFFMAN, Lucinda (Knight) - b 4 Dec 1830; dt John and
Sarah (Meredith) Knight; 23 Sep 1850 m Thomas J. Huffman;
f mbr Mississinewa MM; d 30 Jul 1855 (1,10,17,29,33,65)

HULLINGER, Dora D. - d 5 Dec 1900 at age 1y (29,37,47)

HUNT, Elizabeth - b 15 May 1804; d 19 Jul 1897 (29)

HUNT, Jabez H. - b 26 Aug 1840; s Thomas and Jane Hunt; m
Cyrena Larrence prior to 6 Feb 1865; widower; mbr Marion
MM; d 11 Feb 1903 (1,7,14,29,30,34,37)

HUTCHINS, Harper - b 8 Oct 1879; s Thomas J. and Nancy J.

(Weasner) Hutchins; prob mbr Deer Creek MM; d 16 Jul 1880 (1,7,29)

JACKSON, Anna J. - b 28 May 1832; dt Jesse and Phebe (St. Clair) Jackson; d 1 Apr 1853 (29,46,59)

JACKSON, Charity - b 22 May 1834; dt Jesse and Phebe (St. Clair) Jackson; d 27 Jan 1856 (29,46,59)

JACKSON, Cynthia (Maynard) - b 11 Sep 1835; 16 Oct 1853 m Iredell Jackson; d 12 Aug 1854 (10,29,46,59)

JACKSON, Jehu - b 30 Dec 1829; s Jesse and Phebe (St. Clair) Jackson; d 12 Jul 1854 (29,46,53)

JACKSON, Mary Jane - b 3 Jan 1839; dt Jesse and Phebe (St. Clair) Jackson; d 8 May 1853 (29,46,59)

JACKSON, Phebe (St. Clair) - b VA 4 Mar 1800; dt James and Rachel St. Clair; Clinton Co., OH 18 Jan 1821 m Jesse Jackson; d 6 May 1853 (29,46,59)

JACKSON, Rebecca - b 7 Sep 1841; dt Jesse and Phebe (St. Clair) Jackson; d 1 Jan 1847 (29,46,59)

JAMES, John, Jr. - b NC 4 Dec 1773; s John James, Sr.; m Mary Snead; d 21 Dec 1853 (23,25,29,46,53,59)

JAMES, Mary (Snead) - b ME 18 Nov 1776; dt Henley and Mary (Burford) Snead; m John James, Jr.; d 5 Mar 1869 (23,25, 29,46,50,53,59)

JAMES, Rachel - b Randolph Co. 9 Dec 1822; dt John and Mary (Snead) James; never m; mbr Christian Ch.; d 30 Mar 1905 (19,23,25,29,37,44,46,50,53,54,59,73)

JAMESON, Leona (Avermon) - b Oct 1873; m 1st George A. McElhaney 10 Dec 1902; m 2nd Frank O. Jameson 17 Apr 1911; f mbr Marion MM; mbr Baptist Ch.; d 1959 (1,15,29,35)

JAQUA, Ethel - dt Moses D. and Hulda (Small) Jaqua; sister of Gus Jaqua; d ca 5 Feb 1929 at age 45 (16,29,37,58)

JAQUA, Hulda (Small) - b 6 Jan 1861; dt Josiah and Nancy J. (Boxell) Small; 15 Apr 1883 m Moses D. Jaqua; d 8 Dec 1893 (11,16,29,46)

JARVIS, Virgil - s Samuel and Ocea (Miller) Jarvis; d ca 24 May 1897 at age 2y (11,16,37)

JAY, infant - s Abijah C. and Caroline (Coffin) Jay; b & d 8 Sep 1868 (1,29,46)

JAY, Abijah Cooper - b Montgomery Co., OH 12 Oct 1838; s Isaac and Rhoda (Cooper) Jay; 1st m 26 Oct 1864 Caroline 'Callie' Coffin (dec 1880); 2nd m 12 Oct 1881 Rhoda J. Davis; att Earlham Coll; mbr Marion MM; d 18 May 1909 (1,7,10,18, 23,24,25,29,31,37,46,50,53,54,59,65,73)

JAY, Amanda Alice (Curtis) - b 1906; m Everett R. Jay 2 Jun 1928; d ca 14 Nov 1965 (29,36,37)

JAY, Anna (Coggeshall) - b Wayne Co. 27 Mar 1834; dt Nathan and Gulie (Shugart) Coggeshall; 31 Jul 1851 m Denny Jay; f mbr Deer Creek Anti-slavery MM; mbr Deer Creek MM; d 15 Nov 1910 (1,10,25,29,31,37,46,49,50,53,59,64,65)

JAY, Arthur E. - b Marion 30 May 1864; s Walter D. and Nancy Jane (Ellis) Jay; 12 Jun 1888 m Flora I. Jordan; mbr IOOF; f mbr Marion MM; d 17 Jan 1957 (1,29,37,46,57,59,73)

JAY, Caroline 'Callie' (Coffin) - b OH 23 Oct 1847; dt Daniel and Patience (Janney) Coffin; 26 Oct 1864 m Abijah C. Jay; mbr Mississinewa MM; d 28 Jun 1880 (1,11,18,23,29,31,46,50, 59,61,65)

JAY, Carl C. - b Grant Co. 1891; s Arthur E. Jay; d ca 5 Dec 1939 (29,37,57,59)

JAY, Cooper - b 16 Mar 1866; s Abijah C. and Caroline 'Callie' (Coffin) Jay ; Dec 1889 m Ida Engle; Earlham Coll grad; mbr Marion MM; d 30 Aug 1890 (1,11,23,29,46,59,65,73)

JAY, Dennis 'Denny' - b Miami Co., OH 20 Mar 1829; s Thomas and Eliza (Wareham) Jay; 31 Jul 1851 m Anna Coggeshall; mbr & Elder, Deer Creek MM; d 16 Jul 1895 (1,12, 18,25,29,37,46,50,53,54,59,64)

JAY, Everett R. - b 6 Jul 1902; s Volney B. and Flora A. (Campbell) Jay; 2 Jun 1928 m Amanda Alice Curtis; mbr Marion MM (1,24,29,36,46,59)

JAY, Flora A. (Campbell) - b Huntington 10 Dec 1873; dt Green N. and Maria (Sears) Campbell; 4 Jul 1901 m Volney B. Jay; mbr Marion MM; d ca 18 Mar 1959 (1,10,15,29,37,46,53,59)

JAY, Flora I. (Jordan) - b 1864; m Arthur E. Jay 12 Jun 1888; d 13 Apr 1937 (29,59)

JAY, Florence - b Mar 1892; dt Abijah C. and Rhoda (Davis) Jay; mbr Marion MM; d 1981 (1,29,46)

JAY, Harvey J. 'Harry' - b 6 Jun 1861; s Denny and Anna (Coggeshall) Jay; 29 Nov 1888 m Mary Alice Harris; mbr Deer Creek MM; d ca 23 Aug 1934 (1,16,24,25,29,37,40,46,59,64)

JAY, Isaac - b Miami Co., OH 19 Feb 1811; s Walter Denny and Mary (Macy) Jay; 30 Dec 1830 m Rhoda Cooper at Mill Creek Friends MH, OH; Recorded Friends Minister; mbr Mississinewa MM; d 15 May 1880 (1,7,18,23,24,25,27,29,30,46,50,54,59,61, 65,71)

JAY, Isaiah - b IN 25 Nov 1854; s Richard and Mary (Cogges-hall) Jay; ca 1880 m Millicent B.; Recorded Friends Minister; mbr Fairmount MM; d ca 30 Jan 1941 (1,29,37,46,50)

JAY, Jesse - b 14 Mar 1825; s James and Lydia (Hollingsworth) Jay; 1st m Rhoda Thomas in Mar 1848; 2nd m Mahala

Gordon 24 Jun 1857 at Center Friends MH, Jonesboro; mbr Mississinewa MM; d 20 Dec 1875 (1,65)

JAY, Mahala (Gordon) - b IN 1 Feb 1836; dt Richard and Susannah (Hiatt) Gordon; at Center Friends MH, Jonesboro, 24 Jun 1857 m Jesse Jay as his 2nd wife; mbr Marion MM; d 24 Feb 1905 (1,19,24,29,37,46,50,53,62)

JAY, Mary (Coggeshall) - b IN 29 Jul 1832; dt Nathan and Gulia (Shugart) Coggeshall; 2 Apr 1852 m Richard Jay; f mbr Deer Creek Anti-slavery MM; mbr Oak Ridge MM; d 28 Jul 1910 (1,10,29,46,49,50,59,65)

JAY, Mary Alice (Harris) - b 19 Sep 1869; dt David S. and Rachel (Wiant) Harris; 29 Nov 1888 m Harvey H. Jay; mbr Deer Creek MM; d ca 11 Aug 1950 (1,16,24,29,37,46,59,64)

JAY, Nathan - b IN 10 Feb 1857; s Richard and Mary (Coggeshall) Jay; mbr Oak Ridge MM; d 4 Sep 1876, may be bur Back Creek Friends Cem (10,29,46,50,59,61)

JAY, Rhoda (Cooper) - b Montgomery Co., OH 28 Feb 1813; dt Isaac and Elizabeth (Kennedy) Cooper; 30 Dec 1830 m Isaac Jay at Mill Creek Friends MH, OH; mbr Marion MM; d 15 Nov 1894 (1,11,18,24,25,29,46,47,50,53,57,59,65,71,73)

JAY, Rhoda J. (Davis) - b IN 13 Apr 1851; dt Jacob O. and Rebecca (Pearson) Davis; 12 Oct 1881 m Abijah C. Jay as his 2nd wife; mbr Marion MM; d ca 8 Dec 1947 (1,8,10,18,23,29,31, 37,50,59,65)

JAY, Richard - b IN 4 Apr 1830; s James and Lydia (Hollingsworth) Jay; 2 Apr 1852 m Mary Coggeshall; mbr & Elder, Oak Ridge MM; d 3 Nov 1874, may be bur Back Creek Friends Cem (1,10,29,46,50,54,59,61)

JAY, Riley - b IN 8 Oct 1852; s Denny and Anna (Coggeshall) Jay; 14 Mar 1872 m Anzonetta 'Nettie' Haisley; mbr South Marion MM; d 8 Oct 1915 (1,10,46,50,64)

JAY, Volney B. - b Grant Co. 5 Apr 1866; s Jesse and Mahala (Gordon) Jay; 4 Jul 1901 m Flora A. Campbell; mbr Marion Friends; d 29 Dec 1911 (1,15,19,24,29,32,37,46,53,59,65)

JAY, Walter Denny - b OH 2 Jan 1835; s Isaac and Rhoda (Cooper) Jay; 17 Oct 1857 m Nancy Jane Ellis; mbr Mississinewa MM; d ca 1871 (1,7,10,18,24,25,29,42,46,50,53,54,59,65)

JONES, Anna (Pearson) - b NC 17 Jan 1792; dt Enoch and Ann (Evans) Pearson; m Obadiah Jones 3 Aug 1820 in Concord Friends MH, OH; mbr & Overseer, Deer Creek Antislavery MM; d 12 Dec 1863 (1,18,23,25,29,30,46,50,53,59,71)

JONES, Annie L. - b 20 Oct 1875; dt M. and C.A. Jones; d 30 Sep 1876 (29)

JONES, Daniel - b 10 Sep 1809; s Daniel and Jemima Jones; m Elizabeth Small; mbr Mississinewa MM; d 30 Jan 1842 (1,29, 52,53,65)

JONES, Elbert - b Feb 1884; s Hiram B. and M.E. Jones; d 8 Nov 1889 (29)

JONES, Francis M. - b IN 11 Oct 1833; s Daniel and Elizabeth (Small) Jones; prob m __ 18 Nov 1857; during CW serv Co. D, 26th Ind. Inf.; mbr Mississinewa MM; d 26 Feb 1926 (1,2, 54,65)

JONES, Harry - d Mar 1895 (29,37)

JONES, Hiram B. - b 5 May 1838; m Mary E.; d 16 Sep 1882 (29)

JONES, Lillie E. 'Tillie' - b 6 Aug 1873; dt Hiram B. and Mary E. Jones; d 18 Oct 1883, may be bur Deer Creek Friends Cem (11,29)

JONES, Obadiah - b NC 31 Oct 1791; s Abijah and Rachel (Harris) Jones; m Anna Pearson 3 Aug 1820 in Concord Friends MH, OH; 1832 came to Grant Co.; f mbr Deer Creek

Anti-slavery MM; d 23 Aug 1856 (1,17,18,23,25,29,30,46,53,59, 71,73)

JONES, Ora E. - b 13 Jun 1861; dt Hiram B. and M.C./E. Jones; d 16 Jul 1879 (29)

JONES, Reuben S. - b 12 Apr 1839; s Daniel and Elizabeth (Small) Jones; m Mary Edgerton; during CW serv as 1st Lieut., Co. A, 68th Ind. Inf.; mbr Marion MM; d 1 Sep 1925 (1,2,29,46,58,59)

JUNKEN, Bosella - b 1832; m James Junken; d 4 Jun 1871 (29)

KANNARD, Milton - d ca 19 Aug 1904 (29,38)

KAUFMAN, Beulah C. (Knight) - b IN 8 Jun 1824; dt Thomas and Christian (Thomas) Knight; was a school tchr; mbr Indianapolis MM; d 12 Feb 1873 (1,22,29,34,50,51,65)

KELLEY, Avis (Sleeper) - b NY 30 Jan 1804; dt Samuel and Patience (Burrough) Sleeper; 3 Feb 1825 m Timothy Kelley; mbr Mississinewa MM; d 15 Jan 1863 (1,18,22,23,29,30,62)

KELLEY, Timothy - b SC 28 Mar 1796; s Samuel and Hannah (Pearson) Kelly; 3 Feb 1825 m Avis Sleeper; mbr Back Creek MM; d 13 Dec 1866 (1,18,22,23,29,30,50)

KING, Isaiah S. - b Jun 1861; s J.T. and E. King; d 6 Oct 1863 (29)

KNIGHT, Christian (Thomas) - b SC 12 Feb 1785; dt John and Molly (Clark) Thomas; 26 Jan 1804 m Thomas Knight, Sr.; mbr Mississinewa MM; d 20 Aug 1836 (1,17,29,46,51,53,55 59,65)

KNIGHT, Fernando F. - b 17 Jun 1860; s James and Rachel (Wilcutts) Knight; mbr Deer Creek MM; d 13 Sep 1879 (1,29, 46,65)

KNIGHT, Hannah J. (Morgan) - b Wayne Co. 20 Jul 1844; dt Thomas and Elizabeth Morgan; 12 Sep 1865 m Jehu/John Knight; mbr South Marion MM; d ca 14 Jul 1910 (1,29,31,38, 50,59,64)

KNIGHT, Hershel M. - b 30 Aug 1866; s Jehu and Hannah J. (Morgan) Knight; 31 Jan 1895 m Laura Mickel; f mbr Deer Creek MM; mbr M.E. Ch.; d ca 11 May 1953 (1,16,29,38,46,53, 59,64,65)

KNIGHT, James 'Jemma' - b NC 14 Apr 1810; s Thomas and Christian (Thomas) Knight; Henry Co. 1st m Mary Chew 26 Oct 1837; 2nd m Rachel Wilcutts; mbr Deer Creek MM; d 12 Apr 1895 (1,7,9,11,12,29,30,38,46,47,50,51,53,54,55,59,65,70)

KNIGHT, Jehu/John - b IN 25 Mar 1841; s Manoah and Martha (Wilcutts) Knight; 12 Sep 1865 m Hannah J. Morgan; mbr Marion MM; d ca 25 Dec 1912 (1,7,29,32,38,46,50,54,59,64,65,73)

KNIGHT, Laura (Mickel) - b Jul 1866; dt Josiah and Elizabeth Mickel; m Hershel M. Knight 31 Jan 1895; d 29 Mar 1923 (16,29,38,46,53,58,59)

KNIGHT, Lydia (Carter) - b IN 28 Jan 1846; dt George and Mary (Buller) Carter; 9 Jul 1870 m Thomas W. Knight; d 9 Apr 1871 (10,25,29,46,50,59)

KNIGHT, Manoah - b 19 Mar 1816; s Thomas and Christian (Thomas) Knight; 24 Mar 1836 m Martha 'Patsy' Wilcuts; mbr Mississinewa MM; d 1 Oct 1854 (1,10,29,46,51,53,55,59,65)

KNIGHT, Martha 'Patsy' (Wilcutts) - b IN 11 Jun 1819; dt Clark Wilcutts; 24 Mar 1836 m Manoah Knight; mbr Deer Creek MM; d 10 Apr 1873 (1,10,29,46,50,53,54,55,59,64,65)

KNIGHT, Rachel (Wilcutts) - b IN 26 Jul 1817; dt Clark Wilcutts; m James 'Jemma' Knight; mbr Deer Creek MM; d 3 Nov 1881 (1,29,46,50,55,59,65)

KNIGHT, Samuel - b IN 7 Aug 1839; s Manoah and Martha 'Patsy' (Wilcutts) Knight; 27 Mar 1858 m Lacy Ann Weasner; Pvt., Co. I, 101st Ind. Inf. during CW; mbr Mississinewa MM; d 21 Jan 1887 (1,10,11,23,24,29,43,46,50,54,65,73)

KNIGHT, Sarah - b 25 Oct 1813; dt Thomas, Sr. and Christian (Thomas) Knight; mbr Mississinewa MM; d 22 Jan 1834 (1,29, 46,51,55,59,65)

KNIGHT, Sarah Ella (Fenstermaker) - b OH 4 Oct 1848; dt George W. and Mary A. Moore Fenstermaker; 31 Dec 1864 m William Knight, Sr.; mbr Marion MM; d 25 Oct 1938 (1,10,29, 38,46,50,59,65)

KNIGHT, Thomas, Sr. - b NC 16 Nov 1781; s Solomon and Elizabeth Knight; 26 Jan 1804 m Christian Thomas; mbr Mississinewa MM; d 11 Aug 1831 (1,17,23,29,46,51,53,55,59,65)

KNIGHT, William - b IN 23 Jun 1842; s Manoah and Martha (Wilcutts) Knight; 31 Dec 1864 m Sarah Ella Fenstermaker; mbr Marion MM; d 13 Jan 1917 (1,7,10,29,38,46,50,54,58,59, 65,73)

LAFFERTY, Cliffie E. (Thomas) - b 1876; dt Isaac and Caroline W. (Lacy) Thomas; m John W. Lafferty 21 Dec 1898; mbr Deer Creek MM; d ca 22 Sep 1919 (1,15,29,38,46)

LAFFERTY, John W. - b 1862; m Cliffie E. Thomas 21 Dec 1898; d Indianapolis 22 Sep 1914 (15,29,38,58)

LAMB, Mary J. - d ca 4 Mar 1941 (29,38)

LANE, Enos R. - b OH 14 Aug 1852; s Julius and Elizabeth (Randall) Lane; 24 Dec 1871 m Susannah B. Wiant; f mbr Mississinewa MM; d ca 7 Oct 1897 (1,10,29,30,38,50,65)

LANE, Harry 'Carvey' - d ca 13 Dec 1898 at age 23y (13,29,38)

LANE, Mary Ann - b 30 Apr 1845; dt Julius and Elizabeth

(Randall) Lane; mbr Mississinewa MM; d 10 Jan 1858 (1,29, 30,65)

LEAPLEY, Almeda (Moore) - b OH 1839; dt William G. Moore; OH m Jacob B. Leapley prior to 1860; d 3 Nov 1915 (25,29,38,53,58,59)

LEAPLEY, Gerald M. - b 1894; s William Leapley; d ca 27 Dec 1946 (29,38,59)

LEAPLEY, Jacob B. - b Shelby Co., OH 29 Mar 1837; OH m Almeda Moore prior to 1860; d ca 11 Sep 1913 (7,25,29,32, 38,59)

LEAPLEY, Mary E. - b 1895; d ca 20 Nov 1974 (29,38)

LEVERTON, Arrena - b 13 Dec 1873; dt John E. and Emaline (Price) Leverton; att Marion Normal Coll; mbr Deer Creek MM; d 8 Dec 1890, funeral in South Marion Friends MH (1,10,11,29)

LEVERTON, Emaline (Price) - b Grant Co. 17 Jul 1852; dt Samuel and Nancy (Poe) Price; 18 Jun 1870 m John E. Leverton; mbr Deer Creek MM; d 20 May 1930 (1,10,29,38, 50,58)

LEVERTON, John E. - b Fayette Co. 19 Nov 1839; s Charles Leverton; m Emaline Price 18 Jun 1870; serv 3rd Ind. Battery during CW; mbr Deer Creek MM; d 7 Apr 1896, funeral in South Marion Friends MH (1,2,7,10,12,29,38,47,54)

LEVERTON, Orda - b 7 Feb 1893; d 7 Feb 1893 (29)

LIPSEY, Bertha - b 26 Sep 1873; dt Oliver G. and Hannah C. (Wright) Lipsey; mbr Mississinewa MM; d 13 Jun 1875 (1,7,10, 29,65)

LLOYD, Sarah J. - b OH 17 Mar 1821; m Thomas Lloyd; d 9 Mar 1864 (29,50)

44   MISSISSINEWA FRIENDS CEMETERY

McCORMICK, Hannah (Hiatt) - b Wayne Co. 12 Dec 1810; dt
William and Elizabeth (Sulgrove) Hiatt; Delaware Co.
19 Aug 1830 m Jacob McCormick; mbr Back Creek MM; d 22
Nov 1872 (1,18,25,29,46,50,59)

McCORMICK, Jacob - b Fayette Co. 11 Jan 1812; s Robert and
Anna (McCormick) McCormick; Delaware Co. 19 Aug 1830
m Hannah Hiatt; d 15 Feb 1872 (11,18,22,25,29,46,50,51,54,59)

McCOY, __ - d ca 8 Jun 1962 (38)

McCOY, Frank P. - b 1869; m Mary E. Chamness 23 Feb 1898;
was a school teacher; d ca 11 Mar 1951 (16,29,38,41)

McCOY, Mary E. (Chamness) - b 3 Apr 1874; dt William S.
and Rebecca J. (Lamb) Chamness; 23 Feb 1898 m Frank P.
McCoy; f mbr Marion MM; mbr Marion M.E. Ch.; d 1912
(1,16,29,33)

McELHANEY, Grace A. - b 1906; dt George A. and Leona
(Avermon) McElhaney; prob mbr Marion MM; d May 1912
(1,15,29,32)

McKINNEY, Jasper R. - b 26 Apr 1847; s Fielding S. and Sarah
Ann (Oppey) McKinney; d 5 Dec 1850 (10,23,24,29,46)

McKINNEY, Josephius - b 20 Mar 1852; s David R. and Emily
Elizabeth (Hogin) McKinney; d 13 Feb 1854 (29,46,59)

McKINNEY, Laura - b 2 Jan 1842; dt Fielding S. and Sarah
Ann (Oppey) McKinney; d 9 Nov 1846 (23,24,29,46)

McKINNEY, Lillia - b 31 Oct 1864; dt Fielding S. and Sarah
Ann (Oppey) McKinney; d 15 Jan 1868 (29,59)

McKINNEY, Lucy - b 6 Mar 1852; dt Fielding S. and Sarah
Ann (Oppey) McKinney; d 7 Mar 1853 (29,59)

McKINNEY, William B. - b 28 May 1850; s David R. and

Emily Elizabeth (Hogin) McKinney; d 23 Jan 1854 (29,46)

McKINSEY, Emily (Thomas) - b IN 21 Apr 1843; dt Noah and Elizabeth (Overman) Thomas; 1st m Isaac Hollingsworth, Jr. 26 Feb 1863; 2nd m William M. McKinsey 13 Sep 1887; mbr Marion MM; d ca 27 May 1926 (1,10,16,29,38,46,50,59,65)

McKINSEY, Dr. William M. - b 1843; m Emily (Thomas) Hollingsworth 13 Sep 1887; serv 17th Ind. Inf. during CW; d Jan 1906, funeral Central Christian Ch. (16,19,29,59)

McMILLAN, Clara - d ca 23 Aug 1959 (29,38)

McNEMAR, Estel C. - b 1893; s C.J. McNemar; m Lillian B.; d ca 5 Aug 1936 (7,29,38,39)

McNEMAR, Lillian B. - b 1897; m Estel C. McNemar; d ca 13 Aug 1946 (7,29,38,39)

MACON, Alison - child of I.L. Macon; d 13 Apr 1895 (12,29,38)

MALOTT, Mary Emma - dt Robert and Millicent (Draper) Malott; mbr Mississinewa MM; d 5 Oct 1873 at age 9y, 11m, 8da (1,10,65)

MART, infant - child of Ernest and Olga Smith (Wilson) Mart; d ca 17 Nov 1911 (15,29,38)

MART, infant - child of Ernest and Olga Smith (Wilson) Mart; d Jun 1921 (15,29)

MART, Etta A./S. - d Apr 1895 (29,38)

MART, Henrietta (Shugart) - b 25 Sep 1865; dt Isaac R. and Ann (Whitson) Shugart; 29 Mar 1884 m Samuel O. Mart; mbr Oak Ridge MM; d 7 Feb 1889 (1,11,29,41,46)

MATTHEWS, Charles - m __; d 19 Nov 1898 at age 66y

(13,29,38,47)

MAXWELL, Mary B. - m Winfield D. Maxwell; d ca 2 Mar 1934 (29,38)

MAXWELL, Winfield D. - m Mary B.; d ca 4 Sep 1935 (29,38)

MEREDITH, Arrilla Matilda (Stott) - b 24 Aug 1854; m James Meredith; mbr Marion MM; d 9 Apr 1914 (1,10,29,38,58,59)

MEREDITH, Beth - d ca 20 Apr 1904 (38)

MEREDITH, James - b SC 10 Jun 1850; 25 Jun 1871 m Arrilla Matilda Stott; mbr Marion MM; d ca 27 Jul 1930 (1,7,10,29,38, 58,59)

MICHAEL, Charley - d ca 1 Sep 1907 (29,38)

MICHAEL, Feeby - b Dec 1873; dt William and Jemima J. (Meeks) Michael(s); d 17 Sep 1878 (10,29)

MICHAEL, Isaac - b 2 Oct 1870; s William and Jemima J. (Meeks) Michael(s); d 7 Oct 1870 (10,29)

MICHAEL, Peter - b MD; 8 May 1845 m Phebe Simpson; d 31 Jan 1896 at age 88, funeral in South Marion Friends MH (10,12,27,29,38,50,53,54)

MICHAEL, William - m Ruth Pyeatte 5 Sep 1896; d 30 Sep 1914 prob at age 68 (16,29,38,58)

MICHAELS, Ada - d 10 Aug 1901 at age 1y (29,38,47)

MICHAELS, Inda - dt William Michaels; d 13 Aug 1902 at age 1m (29,38,47)

MICHAELS, William - child of M & M Will Michaels; d 27 Nov 1904 (14,29,38)

MILLER, Alfred - b 24 Nov 1849; d 5 Aug 1887 (29)

MILLER, Earl - s William Miller; d ca 3 Apr 1896 at age 2y (12,29,38)

MILLER, Floyd 'Tommie' - s M & M Robert Miller; d 10 Jan 1899 at age 3y (13,29,38,47)

MILLER, Hilda Frances - dt M & M Robert Miller; d 29 Jul 1900 at age 5m (13,29,38,47)

MILLER, Jacob - d ca 9 Oct 1896 (12,29,38)

MILLER, James - d 13 Aug 1855 (29)

MILLER, Peter - may be - m __; d 4 Jan 1893 (11,29)

MILLER, Robert - m __; d 16 Nov 1902 at age 47 (14,29,38,47)

MILLS, Elizabeth (Willcuts) - d 2 Sep 1895 (12,29,38); prob b 15 May 1829; dt Clark Willcuts; 6 Oct 1851 m Job S. Mills; mbr Mississin-ewa MM (1,10,65)

MILLS, Lydia A. - b Randolph Co. 12 Sep 1862; dt John and Mary J. Mills; d 20 Mar 1881 (11,29)

MILLS, Mary Jane (Mills) - b IN 11 Jun 1843; prob dt Amasa and Susannah (Thomas) Mills; 1st m William H. Porter 29 Oct 1875; 2nd m John Mills; mbr Mississinewa MM; d 1881 (1,10,29,50,59)

MILLS, Naomi - b Wayne Co. 22 Sep 1846; dt Curtis and Sarah Mills; f mbr Marion MM; d Feb ca 17 1907 (1,19,29,38, 50,54,65)

MODLIN, infant - child of Frank and Myrtle (Kannard) Modlin; d ca 27 Oct 1899 (16,29,38)

MODLIN, infant - child of Frank and Myrtle (Kannard)

Modlin; d ca 26 Dec 1909 (16,29,38)

MODLIN, infant - child of Frank and Myrtle (Kannard)
Modlin; d 5 Dec 1901 (16,29,38)

MODLIN, infant - child of Frank and Myrtle (Kannard)
Modlin; b and d 8 Jul 1915 (16,29,38,58)

MODLIN, Betty - d ca 24 Aug 1923 (29,38)

MODLIN, Dillon - b Randolph Co., NC 12 May 1813; s George
and Sarah (Peele) Modlin; 1816 moved to Wayne Co., IN; 1st
m Henry Co. 16 Jan 1834 Elizabeth Draper; 1837 moved to
Grant Co.; 2nd m 9 Jan 1867 Amy (Hunt) McFadden, dt Uriah
and Rebecca Hunt; 3rd m 8 Jul 1880 Elizabeth Hiatt; mbr
Mississinewa MM; d 22 Jun 1897 (1,7,10,12,24,25,29,38,46,54,
57,59,65)

MODLIN, Elizabeth (Draper) - b 25 May 1817; dt Jessie and
Delpha Draper; m Dillon Modlin 16 Jan 1834; mbr Mississinewa MM; d 16 Sep 1865 (1,24,29,46,59,65)

MODLIN, Frank - d ca 8 Mar 1906 (29,38)

MODLIN, Harlan - b 1 Jul 1861; s Reuben and Nancy (Harlen)
Modlin; m Ida May Cain 14 Oct 1891; f mbr Deer Creek MM;
d 15 Mar 1907 (1,16,19,29,38,59)

MODLIN, Joseph - s Franklin H. and Myrtle (Kannard) Modlin; b & d 22 Jan 1917 (16,29,38,46,58)

MODLIN, Martha - dt Franklin H. and Myrtle (Kannard)
Modlin; b & d 15 May 1914 (16,29,38,46)

MODLIN, Mary E. - b 1908; dt Franklin H. and Myrtle (Kannard) Modlin; d 18 Jan 1922 (16,29,38,46)

MODLIN, William - b Grant Co. 16 Oct 1839; s Dillon and
Elizabeth (Draper) Modlin; 21 Aug 1862 m Jane Benbow, dt

MISSISSINEWA FRIENDS CEMETERY

Aaron and Catherine (Elliott) Benbow; f mbr Deer Creek
MM; d 8 Aug 1897 (1,10,12,24,25,29,46,47,54,57,59,64,65)

MOON, Mary Ann (Overman) - b 20 Jan 1872; dt David and
Elizabeth C. (Welch) Overman; 10 Aug 1899 m Rev. Oscar
Moon; mbr Union MM, OH; d 6 Oct 1905 (1,19,29,38,46,59)

MOON, Thomas X. - b Clinton Co., OH 5 Jun 1843; s Isaiah
and Mary Moon; m 1st Almira J.; 19 Jul 1904 m 2nd Carrie
Hadley; during CW serv Co. D, 139th Ind. Inf.; mbr Marion
MM; d 12 Jun 1929 (1,2,15,29,50,54,58,59)

MOORE, Dr. Charles Verling - b Montgomery Co. 1849; s
Jacob and Tacy (Butler) Moore; 2 Sep 1874 m Mary W. Baldwin in Fairmount Friends MH; att Earlham Coll; grad
Medical Univ, Louisville, KY 1878; mbr Fairmount MM;
mbr Grant County Medical Society; d 26 Apr 1897 (1,12,22,24,
25,29,41,42,46,47,50,59)

MOORE, Fred - d ca 12 Oct 1909 (29,38)

MOORE, Harry - d 9 Jan 1889 (29)

MOORE, Mary W. (Baldwin) - b IN 15 Oct 1843; dt Thomas
and Lydia (Thomas) Baldwin; 2 Sep 1874 m Dr. Charles V.
Moore in Fairmount Friends MH; mbr Fairmount MM; d 8
May 1897 (1,12,22,23,24,25,25,29,41,46,47,50,59,65)

MOREHEAD, Claudie - b 25 Sep 1879; d 9 Dec 1887 (29)

MOREHEAD, Elsa - b 17 Nov 1887; d 18 Aug 1888 (29)

MOREHEAD, Emma J. 'Jennie' - b 11 Nov 1869; 2nd wife of
Oliver H.P. Morehead; d 17 Feb 1895, funeral in Marion
Friends MH (12,29)

MOREHEAD, Hazel - b 15 Jun 1893; dt Oliver H.P. Morehead;
d 4 Feb 1894 (11,29)

MOREHEAD, Kate (Carroll) - b 17 Jan 1854; 14 Oct 1875 m
Oliver H.P. Morehead as his 1st wife; mbr Deer Creek MM; d
20 May 1888 (1,11,29)

MORRIS, Aaron - b 4 Jan 1797 or b 1 Jan 1791; s Thomas and
Sarah (Musgrove) Morris; 25 Nov 1819 m Nancy 'Nanny'
Thomas in New Garden Friends MH; mbr White River MM;
d 11 Jun 1832 (8,29,46,51,55,59)

MORRIS, Anny - prob Anna, dt Aaron and Nancy (Thomas)
Morris; b 19 Apr 1823; mbr White River MM (8,29,51)

MORRIS, Caleb - b SC 17 Mar 1801; s Thomas and Sarah
(Musgrove) Morris; Wayne Co. 29 Jan 1820 m Mary 'Polly'
Conner; mbr M.E. Ch.; d 10 Mar 1858 (22,23,27,29,59); may be
bur Griffin Cem (46,53)

MORRIS, Charity - b 1 Oct 1832; dt Nathan and Miriam
(Benbow) Morris; mbr Mississinewa MM; d 13 Nov 1833
(1,29,65)

MORRIS, Daniel - mbr Mississinewa MM; d 10 Jun 1865 at
age 34y, 8m, 2da (1,65)

MORRIS, Ida A. (Leapley) - b Montgomery Co., OH 6 Dec
1859; dt Jacob and Almeda Leapley; 1 Nov 1879 m Luther
Morris; d 8 Nov 1881 (10,11,25,29,46,59)

MORRIS, John - b 18 Feb 1835; s Nathan and Miriam (Benbow) Morris; mbr Mississinewa MM; d 5 Sep 1854 (1,29,46,
59,65)

MORRIS, Lizzy - m __; d ca 27 Sep 1909 at age 55 (29,31,38)

MORRIS, Lucinda J. 'Janey' (Harrell) - b 1856; 22 Jun 1878 m
Orlistus W. Morris; d 29 Dec 1923 (10,29,38,58)

MORRIS, Mary Ann - b 3 Feb 1830; m W.W. Morris; d 30 Jan
1895, funeral in Bethel Friends MH (12,29,38)

MORRIS, Nancy 'Nanny' (Thomas) - b 27 Oct 1800; dt John and Lydia (Snead) Thomas; 25 Nov 1819 m Aaron Morris in New Garden Friends MH; mbr White River MM; d 2 Mar 1832 (8,46,55,59)

MORRIS, Dr. Orlistus W. - b 23 Aug 1855; s Benjamin F. and Ruth (Thomas) Morris; 22 Jun 1878 m Lucinda J. Harrell; f mbr Marion MM; d Elwood 8 May 1909 (1,10,29,31,38,46,64)

MORRIS, Ruth - b 3 Jun 1836; dt Nathan and Miriam (Benbow) Morris; mbr Mississinewa MM; d 6 Sep 1854 (1,25,25,29, 46,59,65)

MORRIS, Thomas - b 31 Dec 1833; s Nathan and Miriam (Benbow) Morris; mbr Mississinewa MM; d 6 Oct 1854 (1,25, 25,29,46,59,65)

MORRIS, William - b 31 Aug 1820; s Aaron and Nancy (Thomas) Morris; 14 Dec 1843 m Margaret Jones; mbr White River MM; d 25 Oct 1851 (8,10,29,53)

MURPHY, Rebecca - b 19 Sep 1815; m Henry N. Murphy; d 1 Sep 1859 (29)

NEAL, Gail B. - b 13 Dec 1886; s Mahlon Fremont and Jeanette (Shugart) Neal; mbr Back Creek MM; d 1978 (1,29,46)

NEAL, Gladys J. - b 20 Nov 1893; dt Mahlon Fremont and Jeanette (Shugart) Neal; grad Jonesboro HS 1910; att Earlham Coll; mbr Back Creek MM; d 1985 (1,29,42,46)

NEAL, Glen W. - b 9 Mar 1884; s Mahlon Fremont and Jeanette (Shugart) Neal; mbr Oak Ridge MM; d 13 Mar 1902, funeral in Christian Ch. (1,14,29,38,46,47)

NEAL, Julia (Presnall) - b NC 3 Apr 1827; dt Nathan and Rebecca (Cox) Presnall; 19 Aug 1847 m William Neal; mbr Back Creek MM; d 5 May 1859 (1,10,17,23,27,29,33,46,59)

NEAL, Mahlon Fremont - b IN 12 Mar 1858; s Mahlon and Maris (Harris) Neal; 24 Nov 1883 m Mary Jeanette 'Nettie' Shugart; mbr Oak Ridge MM; d ca 3 Jun 1925 (1,16,29,38,46, 50,58)

NEAL, Mary B. - b 1890; d 1980 (29)

NEAL, Mary Jeanette 'Nettie' (Shugart) - b 8 Jan 1864; dt William C. and Martha (Steed) Shugart; 24 Nov 1883 m Mahlon Fremont Neal; mbr Oak Ridge MM; d ca 18 Feb 1930 (1,16,29,38,42,46,58)

OCHILTREE, Nora G. (Knight) - b 22 Jan 1866; dt William and Sarah Ella (Fenstermaker) Knight; 10 May 1892 m John C. Ochiltree; f mbr Marion MM; mbr First Presbyterian Ch., Dayton, OH; d ca 27 Apr 1947 (1,16,29,38,46,59,65)

O'NEIL, Gulia/Julia A. (Coggeshall) - b 2 May 1880; dt Eli and Anna (Bogue) Coggeshall; m George B. O'Neill 19 May 1903; mbr Marion MM; d 4 Jun 1914 (1,15,29,46,53)

ORRELL, Helen L. - b 10 Aug 1910; m Hugh R. Orrell; d 14 Sep 1989 (29)

ORRELL, Hugh Roberts - b 25 Sep 1901; m Helen L.; d 29 Jul 1970 (29,38)

OVERMAN, infant - s Anderson C. and Mary E. (Jay) Overman; b & d 30 Jan 1866 (1,29,46)

OVERMAN, infant - s Anderson C. and Mary E. (Jay) Overman; b & d 26 Oct 1867 (1,29,46)

OVERMAN, infant - dt Anderson C. and Mary E. (Jay) Overman; b & d 8 Sep 1869 (1,29,46)

OVERMAN, infant - child of Dr. Charles J. and Effie (Woody) Overman; mbr Marion MM; d ca 14 Apr 1897 (1,12,29,38)

OVERMAN, infant - child of Turner W. and Mary (Stout) Overman; d ca 22 Aug 1897 (16,29,38,46)

OVERMAN, Alhambra - b 18 Jan 1876; s Anderson C. and Mary E. (Jay) Overman; att Earlham Coll; d 1 Jan 1908 (1,24, 25,29,31,38,46,59,65)

OVERMAN, Allen J. - b IN 18 Feb 1853; s Joel and Mary (Smith) Overman; 4 Nov 1875 m Arminta O. Shields; mbr Marion MM; d 26 Aug 1919 (1,7,10,23,24,25,29,38,42,46,50,58, 59,65)

OVERMAN, Amanda Melvina (Hutchins) - b IN 27 Nov 1846; dt David and Amanda Hutchins; 31 Oct 1861 m Joseph H. Overman; mbr Marion MM; d ca 15 Aug 1916 (1,10,13,29, 38,46,50,53,58,65)

OVERMAN, Anderson C. - b IN 12 Feb 1838; s John and Ann (McCracken) Overman; at Mississinewa Friends MH 25 Feb 1863 m Mary Elizabeth Jay; was a surveyor; mbr Mississinewa MM; d 26 Mar 1880 (1,7,24,25,29,46,54,59,61,62,65)

OVERMAN, Ann (McCracken) - b NC 21 Feb 1820; dt David and Elizabeth (Hodgin) McCracken; at Mississinewa Friends MH 24 Dec 1836 m John Overman; mbr Mississinewa MM; d 21 Feb 1865 (1,8,17,23,24,29,50,59,65)

OVERMAN, Arminta O. (Shields) - b IN 12 May 1854; dt John and Arminta (Wroe) Shields; 4 Nov 1875 m Allen J. Overman; mbr Marion MM; d 9 Sep 1924 (1,10,24,29,38,46,50 59,65)

OVERMAN, Barion - child of Turner W. and Mary (Stout) Overman; d 29 Jul 1901 (14,16,29,38,46)

OVERMAN, Callie May - b 12 Nov 1874; dt Isaac S. and Eva (Coffin) Overman; f mbr Marion MM; mbr Marion 1st M.E. Ch.; d ca 2 Apr 1899, funeral in Marion Friends MH (1,13,29, 38,46,65)

OVERMAN, Calvin J. - b IN 17 May 1836; s Silas and Johannah (James) Overman; m Sarah Ann King 18 Feb 1857; f mbr Mississinewa MM; serv Co. B, 8th Ind. Inf. until d Indianapolis 5 Jun 1861 (1,10,11,23,29,46,50)

OVERMAN, Clarkson D. - b Grant Co. 1 Apr 1851; s John and Ann (McCracken) Overman; 13 Feb 1873 m Isabella Wright in Mississinewa Friends MH; att Marion Normal; mbr Fairmount MM; d ca 18 Feb 1933 (1,7,24,25,29,38,40,46,50,53,59,65)

OVERMAN, David - b Grant Co. 20 Jan 1840; s John and Ann (McCracken) Overman; 3 Feb 1864 m Elizabeth C. Welch at Miami MH, OH; 1885 - 1889, Marion Postmaster; mbr Marion MM; d 10 Jun 1906 (1,7,19,23,24,25,29,30,38,44,46,50,59,62,65,73)

OVERMAN, David G. - b 1893; s Eugene and Leona (Miller) Overman; mbr Marion MM; d 19 Apr 1895 (1,12,16,29,38, 46,47)

OVERMAN, Delight - b 5 Aug 1877; dt George B. and Mary J. (Jones) Overman; mbr Marion MM; d 17 Sep 1898 (1,13,29,46, 47,59,65)

OVERMAN, Eli - b NC 16 Feb 1785; s Ephraim and Rachel B. (Small) Overman; 4 Nov 1812 m Polly Thomas in Whitewater Friends MH; 1827 came to Grant Co.; mbr Mississinewa MM; d 22 Apr 1855 (1,11,23,24,25,29,46,55,59,65)

OVERMAN, Elizabeth (Hall) - b 20 Feb 1804; dt Joseph and Miriam Hall; 19 Dec 1822 m Reuben Overman at New Garden MH; mbr Mississinewa MM; d 2 Oct 1852 (1,8,29,46, 62,65)

OVERMAN, Elizabeth (Jones) - b 1830; 4 Jun 1851 m Ephraim C. Overman; may be mbr Marion MM; d ca 31 Dec 1913 (1,10, 29,34,38)

OVERMAN, Elizabeth Cooper (Welch) - b Warren Co., OH 30 Aug 1836; dt Webster G. and Mary (Cooper) Welch; 3 Feb

1864 m David Overman; mbr Marion MM; d 25 Nov 1916 (1,18,23,29,30,46,58,59,62,73)

OVERMAN, Emily A. (Baldwin) - b IN 9 Dec 1847; dt Dillon and Mary (Rice) Baldwin; m Lindley M. Overman 11 Mar 1869; f mbr Marion MM; d 25 Mar 1904 (1,10,14,29,38,46,50)

OVERMAN, Ephraim - b NC 11 Jun 1790; s Ephraim and Rachel B. (Small) Overman; Wayne Co. 13 Dec 1817 m Miriam Draper; mbr Mississinewa MM; d 12 May 1852 (1,23, 24,25,29,46,53,59,62,65,72)

OVERMAN, Ephraim C. - b OH 22 Sep 1819; s Eli and Polly (Thomas) Overman; 29 Jul 1841 m 1st Martha Ann Jones; m 2nd Elizabeth Jones 4 Jun 1851; mbr Marion MM; d 15 Feb 1895 (1,7,10,11,12,24,25,29,34,38,46,50,59,65)

OVERMAN, Eugene W. - b 30 Mar 1867; s David and Elizabeth C. (Welch) Overman; 3 Apr 1892 m Leona C. Miller; mbr Marion MM; d 10 May 1896 (1,7,12,16,23,24,29,38,46,47,59)

OVERMAN, Eunice - b 7 Feb 1827; dt Reuben and Elizabeth (Hall) Overman; mbr Mississinewa MM; d 18 Sep 1828 (1,29, 46,65)

OVERMAN, Eva (Coffin) - b OH 31 Oct 1852; dt Daniel and Patience Coffin; 13 Mar 1873 m Isaac S. Overman; mbr Marion MM; d 1 Apr 1923 (1,10,29,38,46,50,58,65)

OVERMAN, George Barclay - b Grant Co. 16 May 1833; s Ephraim and Miriam (Draper) Overman; 20 Jul 1853 m Mary J. Jones in Mississinewa Friends MH; mbr Marion MM; d 17 Jun 1908 (1,7,23,24,25,29,31,46,50,54,59,65,73)

OVERMAN, Isaac - b 4 Jul 1832; s Reuben and Elizabeth (Hall) Overman; mbr Mississinewa MM; d 25 Jul 1833 (1,65)

OVERMAN, Isaac Jay - b 28 Oct 1863; s Anderson C. and Mary E. (Jay) Overman; mbr Mississinewa MM; d 12 Apr 1875 (1,24,

25,29,59,61,65)

OVERMAN, Isaac S. - b IN 15 Dec 1847; s Joel and Mary (Smith) Overman; 13 Mar 1873 m Eva Coffin; mbr Marion MM; d ca 1 Mar 1922 (1,7,10,23,24,25,29,38,46,50,54,58,59,65)

OVERMAN, Isabelle S. (Wright) - b IN 2 Aug 1850; dt Joab and Malinda (Elliott) Wright; 13 Feb 1873 m Clarkson D. Overman; mbr Fairmount MM; d 5 Oct 1924 (1,24,25,29,38, 46,50,58,59)

OVERMAN, Jesse - b Wayne Co. 30 Nov 1817; s Eli and Polly (Thomas) Overman; 21 Feb 1839 m Sarah 'Sally' Clark; mbr Mississinewa MM; d 22 Sep 1855 (1,10,24,25,46,59,65)

OVERMAN, Joel - b Randolph Co. 11 May 1822; s Eli and Polly (Thomas) Overman; 20 Oct 1841 m Mary Smith at Mississinewa Friends MH; mbr Marion MM; d 19 Oct 1901 (1,7,11,14,23,24,25,29,38,46,47,50,54,56,59,65,73)

OVERMAN, John - b Randolph Co. 21 Mar 1816; s Eli and Polly (Thomas) Overman; 24 Dec 1836 m Ann McCracken in Mississinewa Friends MH; mbr Mississinewa MM; d 13 Aug 1875 (1,23,24,25,29,46,50,54,59,65)

OVERMAN, John A. - b 16 Oct 1874; s David and Elizabeth C. (Welch) Overman; mbr Mississinewa MM; d 20 Jun 1876 (1,29,46)

OVERMAN, Joseph - b IN 8 Sep 1841; s Jesse and Sarah (Clark) Overman; 15 Nov 1866 m Almira A. Newby; during CW serv as Corp., Co. K, 118th Ind. Inf.; prob dismissed by Mississinewa MM; d 12 Apr 1924 (1,2,10,24,29,46,50,54,58, 59,65)

OVERMAN, Joseph H. - b IN 19 Sep 1840; s Reuben and Elizabeth Overman; 31 Oct 1861 m Amanda M. Hutchins; mbr South Marion MM; d 14 Mar 1900, funeral in South Marion Friends MH (7,10,13,29,38,46,47,50,53,54,65,73)

OVERMAN, Lindley Murray - b Grant Co. 1 May 1845; s Joel and Mary (Smith) Overman; 1st m Emily A. Baldwin 11 Mar 1869; 2nd m Luanna Phillips 4 Sep 1905; att Earlham Coll; was a tchr; f mbr Marion MM; mbr Baptist Ch.; d 13 Nov 1909 (1,10,15,23,24,25,29,31,46,50,59,65)

OVERMAN, Lydia (Rue) - b Wayne Co. 18 Oct 1828; dt Henry and Rebecca (Talbot) Rue; in Whitewater Friends MH 31 Dec 1845 m Ephraim Overman, s Jesse and Keziah; mbr Mississinewa MM; d May 1847 (1,9,46)

OVERMAN, Malinda B. (Draper) - b IN 1 May 1851; dt David and Elizabeth Draper; prior to 5 Jun 1869 m Nathan P. Overman; mbr Mississinewa MM; d 31 Aug 1876 (1,29,50,61)

OVERMAN, Mary (Smith) - b West Elkton, Preble Co., OH 3 Oct 1826; dt Jesse and Martha (Randall) Smith; m Joel Overman 20 Oct 1841 in Mississinewa Friends MH; mbr Marion MM; d 28 Aug 1900 (1,13,23,24,29,38,46,47,50,59,65,73)

OVERMAN, Mary - b 18 Sep 1830; dt Reuben and Elizabeth (Hall) Overman; mbr Mississinewa MM; d 27 May 1833 (1,65)

OVERMAN, Mary Ann - b IN 2 Oct 1858; dt Joel and Mary (Smith) Overman; mbr Mississinewa MM; d 5 Nov 1864 (1,24,46,50,59,62,65)

OVERMAN, Mary J. (Jones) - b IN 11 Mar 1836; dt Daniel and Elizabeth (Small) Jones; 20 Jul 1853 m George B. Overman; mbr Marion MM; d 16 Dec 1919 (1,23,29,38,42,46,50,58,59,65)

OVERMAN, Milton - b IN 22 Aug 1845; s Jesse and Sarah (Clark) Overman; 28 Apr 1868 m Mary Powell; 1868 disowned by Mississinewa MM because he serv Co. D, 153rd Ind. Inf. during CW; d 5 Jun 1929 (1,2,10,23,29,46,50,54,59,65)

OVERMAN, Miriam (Draper) - b NC 13 Sep 1799; dt Josiah and Miriam Draper; Wayne Co. 13 Dec 1817 m Ephraim Overman; mbr Mississinewa MM; d 19 Mar 1854 (1,23,29,46,

53,59,65,72)

OVERMAN, Nathan P. - b IN 1844; s Reuben and Elizabeth (Hall) Overman; m 1st Malinda B. Draper prior to 5 Jun 1869; 12 Mar 1881 m 2nd Sarah Jane 'Jennie' Stallings; d 27 Mar 1910, funeral in South Marion Friends MH (1,10,24,29,31,38, 46,50,54,59,73)

OVERMAN, Polly (Thomas) - b Rockingham Co., NC 19 Dec 1792; dt John and Lydia (Snead) Thomas; 4 Nov 1812 m Eli Overman in Whitewater Friends MH; mbr Mississinewa MM; d 5 Nov 1880 (1,11,23,25,29,46,50,54,55,59,65)

OVERMAN, Polly (Moorman) - b 23 Aug 1815; dt Uriah and Hannah (Mendenhall) Moorman; 18 Aug 1836 m Stephen Overman in Mississinewa Friends MH; mbr Mississinewa MM; d 10 Jan 1851 (1,9,17,24,29,46,65)

OVERMAN, Rachel - b 27 Apr 1842; dt John and Ann (McCracken) Overman; mbr Mississinewa MM; d 18 Oct 1848 (1,24,29,46,59,65)

OVERMAN, Robert B. - b 11 Mar 1844; d 5 Jan 1848 (29)

OVERMAN, Sarah Jane (Modlin) - b 12 Dec 1849; dt Dillon and Elizabeth (Draper) Modlin; 21 Oct 1875 m Willis Overman; mbr Marion MM; d ca 7 Mar 1917 (1,7,10,29,38,46,58,65)

OVERMAN, Silas - b 28 Mar 1829; s Reuben and Elizabeth (Hall) Overman; mbr Mississinewa MM; d 27 Jul 1833 (1,65)

OVERMAN, Stephen - b IN 6 Sep 1814; s Eli and Polly (Thomas) Overman; 18 Aug 1836 m 1st Polly Moorman in Mississinewa Friends MH; 24 Mar 1852 m 2nd Sarah Small in Mississinewa Friends MH; mbr Mississinewa MM; d 30 Oct 1877 (1,24,25,29,46,50,54,59,62,65)

OVERMAN, Thomas Ellwood - mbr Mississinewa MM; d 17 Jul 1853 at age 4m, 27da (65)

OVERMAN, Turner W. - b 23 Dec 1864; s David and Elizabeth C. (Welch) Overman; 28 Jun 1883 m Mary Stout; mbr Mississinewa MM; d after Jun 1906 (1,7,16)

OVERMAN, Walter D. - b IN 24 Aug 1854; s George B. and Mary J. (Jones) Overman; 24 Dec 1878 m Sarah Ansro Mills; mbr Mississinewa MM; d 27 Oct 1879 (1,10,11,23,29,46,50,59, 61,65)

OVERMAN, William - b IN 7 Mar 1842; s Stephen and Polly (Moorman) Overman; during CW serv Co. A, 75th Ind. Inf.; mbr Mississinewa MM; d (1,2,24,29,50,65)

OVERMAN, Willis - b IN 22 Sep 1838; s Reuben and Elizabeth (Hall) Overman; 21 Oct 1875 m Sarah Jane Modlin in Mississinewa Friends MH; mbr Mississinewa MM; d 18 Mar 1885 (1,10,29,46,50,54,61)

PAINTER, Evelyn E. - dt J.A. Painter; d ca 8 Oct 1922 (29,38)

PALMER, infant - d ca 17 Apr 1915 (29,38)

PANNELL, Myrtle - d ca 9 Sep 1897 (29,38)

PARNELL, Deliah - d ca 26 Mar 1901 (29,38)

PEACOCK, Sarah - b 12 Feb 1840; dt John and Abigail (Baldwin) Peacock; mbr Mississinewa MM; d 9 Oct 1854 (1,65)

PEARSON, Lillie Gertrude (Newbern) - b Feb 1870; dt Paul and Eliza E. (Horn) Newbern; m Charles M. Pearson; mbr Marion MM; d 4 Mar 1894 (1,7,9,29,61)

PEARSON, Rachel - b 9 Oct 1850; dt Hiram and Charity C. (Hollingsworth) Pearson; mbr Mississinewa MM; d 20 Dec 1852 (1,65)

PEARSON, Ruth (Oren) - b TN Jan 1807; dt John and Ruth Oren; 17 Apr 1840 m Joseph Pearson in Dover Friends MH,

OH; f mbr Deer Creek Anti-slavery MM; d 6 Jun 1865 (1,29,30, 46,50)

PEARSON, Thomas - s Joseph and Ruth (Oren) Pearson; mbr Deer Creek Anti-slavery MM; d 5 Dec 1847 (1,29,46)

PEEBLES, Sarah A. (Small) - b 9 Aug 1820; 1st m Enoch Yates 1839; 2nd m Jacob Lamm 26 Mar 1850; 3rd m ca Dec 1868 John E. Peebles (dec 1885); mbr Marion MM; d 6 Feb 1898, funeral in South Marion Friends MH (1,10,13,29,38,73)

PEGG, Sarah (Griffin) - b 1770; dt James and Hannah (Kenyon) Griffin; 1st m Gideon Small (dec 4 Mar 1811); 2nd m Valentine Pegg 4 Apr 1821 at Whitewater Friends MH; mbr Mississinewa MM; d 1853 (1,9,17,29,30,33)

PENCE, Dora C. - b 1865; s Darius and Massey Jane 'Mary' (Harter) Pence; m Gertrude M. Leapley 18 Aug 1897; d 7 Sep 1949 (10,16,24,29,38,59)

PENCE, Gertrude M. (Leapley) - dt Jacob B. and Almeda (Moore) Leapley; m Dora C. Pence 18 Aug 1897; d 28 Mar 1946 (16,29,38,53,59)

PETERS, Charles C. - b 1880; s Orange E. and Rosella J. (Cammack) Peters; mbr Marion MM; d 6 Apr 1904 (1,14,25,29,38,59)

PETERS, Orange E. - b IN ca 1855; s Samuel Peters; 1 Feb 1877 m Rosella J. Cammack; f mbr Marion MM; d ca 17 Aug 1925 (1,10,25,29,38,50,53,59)

PETERS, Rosella J. (Cammack) - b IN 1857; dt Willis and Sarah (Jay) Cammack; 1 Feb 1877 m Orange E. Peters; f mbr Marion MM; d 26 Jul 1921 (1,7,10,24,25,29,38,50,53,58,59)

PICKETT, Susannah (Thomas) - b 25 May 1819; dt Elijah and Susanna (Snead) Thomas; m 1st Amasa Mills; KS m 2nd Caleb Pickett 19 Nov 1881; mbr Marion MM; d 26 Feb 1904 (14,29,38,59)

PIERCE, Amanda - b 18 Aug 1857; dt G. and L. Pierce; d 4 Sep 1859 (29)

PIERCE, Elizabeth Ann (Kendall) - b IN 15 Sep 1842; 17 Feb 1870 m George W. Pierce as his 2nd wife; mbr Fairmount MM; d 6 Jan 1872 (1,10,29,50)

PINER, Garland - s M & M John Piner; d 3 Mar 1898 at age 4m (13,29,38)

PINER, Harry - s M & M John Piner; d ca 15 Sep 1895 (12,29,38)

PLUMMER, James M. - b 18 Jan 1850; d 20 Feb 1872 (29)

POE, Elizabeth (Lloyd) - b Guilford Co., NC 25 Dec 1800; m Gabriel P. Poe; d 29 Apr 1878 (25,29,50,59)

POE, Elmina - b 9 Dec 1844; m William D. Poe; d 17 May 1864 (29)

POE, Gabriel P. - b Guilford Co., NC 1 Nov 1794; m Elizabeth Lloyd; d 2 Jun 1872 (25,29,50,54,59)

POE, Sarah - b 30 Oct 1859; dt John D. and Sarah (Philips) Poe; d 31 Dec 1860 (10,29)

POWNELL, Ernest Arlie - b 1894; s Wesley Pownell/Pownall; mbr Marion MM; d ca 12 Feb 1920 (1,29,38)

POWNELL, Hannah - 1st m Joseph Hammond; 22 Jul 1905 m 2nd William Pownell; f mbr Marion MM; mbr W.M. Ch.; d 5 Nov 1923 at age 74 (1,14,15,29,33,38,58)

POWNELL, Mary E. (Hallenback) - b 1894; 3 Jun 1914 m Ernest Arlie Pownell; d Nov 1979 (29,35)

POWNELL, Viola Frances (Hammond) - b 1871; dt Joseph and Hannah Hammond; 25 Dec 1887 m Wesley Giran

Pownell; f mbr Duck Creek MM; mbr Marion MM; d ca 5 Dec 1940 (1,7,16,29,33,38)

POWNELL, Wesley C. - may be s William Pownell (58); d ca 7 Apr 1933 (29,38,40)

POWNELL, Wesley Giran - b 1866; 25 Dec 1887 m Viola F. Hammond; mbr Marion MM; d ca 12 Mar 1942 (1,16,29,38)

PRICE, Mary Ann (Marshall) - b IN 27 Sep 1850; dt Joshua and Tamer (Osborn) Marshall; 24 Nov 1870 m John W. Price; mbr Deer Creek MM; d 2 Jul 1879 (1,10,29,50,59,65)

PRICE, Phyllis J. - b 1929; d 25 Feb 1980 (29)

PUCKETT, Aubry - 21 Jun 1915 m Helen Haines; d 9 Jan 1918 at age 22 (29,35,38,58)

PUTNAM, John - b 16 Jun 1839; d 26 Jul 1888 (29)

RANDALL, Walter W. - b 1879; drowned ca 21 Apr 1936 (29,39)

RATLIFF, Cornelius S. - b IN 11 May 1829; s Joseph and Sarah (Shugart) Ratliff; 1834 came to Grant Co. from Wayne Co.; m Susan Jay 19 Sep 1855 at Center Friends MH, Jonesboro; mbr Mississinewa MM; killed by horse 2 May 1882 (1,7, 8,9,11,22,24,25,29,33,41,46,50,51,53,54,56,59,61,65)

RATLIFF, Emma L. (Knight) - b Madison Co.; dt Samuel and Lacy Ann (Weesner) Knight; 4 Feb 1881 m Charles L. Ratliff (dec Jan 1898); f mbr Marion MM; d ca 7 Mar 1933 (1,10,24,29, 38,40,46,59)

RATLIFF, Grace Belle - dt Charles L. and Emma L. (Knight) Ratliff; d ca 5 May 1961 (24,29,38,40,46,59)

RATLIFF, John - b Wayne Co. 1 Mar 1822; s Joseph and Sarah (Shugart) Ratliff; m Sarah Pearson 20 Dec 1848 at Mississinewa Friends MH; att Franklin Coll 2 yrs.; f mbr Ind. State Legislature; mbr Marion MM; d 27 Feb 1912 (1,7,24,25,27,29, 32,38,43,46,50,51,53,54,56,59,62)

RATLIFF, John - b 25 Jul 1892; s Levi D. and Belle (Hix) Ratliff; d 4 Jul 1904 (14,29,38,46,56)

RATLIFF, Olla - b 9 Feb 1878; dt Nela H. and Susannah (Thomas) Ratliff; d 3 Sep 1883 (11,46)

RATLIFF, Sarah (Pearson) - b Henry Co. 7 Dec 1827; dt Levi and Huldah (Thomas) Pearson; m John Ratliff 20 Dec 1848 at Mississinewa Friends MH; Recorded Friends Minister; mbr Marion MM; d ca 10 May 1912 (1,24,27,29,32,38,43,46,50,59, 62,65)

RATLIFF, Susan (Jay) - b Miami Co., OH 9 Oct 1830; dt Denny and Mary Jay; 19 Sep 1855 m Cornelius Ratliff at Back Creek Friends MH; Recorded Friends Minister; mbr Fairmount MM; d Danville, IL 22 Mar 1904 (1,14,22,27,29,30,38,46,50, 56,65)

RATLIFF, Verlin - b 30 Jan 1880; s Harvey and Elizabeth (Knight) Ratliff; mbr Deer Creek MM; d 11 Jul 1880 (1,29,46)

REEVES, Sampson - b NC 24 Nov 1815; m Sarah Ann Conner 1 Nov 1838; W.M. Minister; d 18 Feb 1879 (7,12,25,27,29, 50,53,54)

REEVES, Sarah Ann (Conner) - b Preble Co., OH 7 or 27 Dec 1822; m Sampson Reeves 1 Nov 1838; moved to IN 1842; mbr W.M. Ch.; d Aug 1896 (12,25,29,50,53)

REYNOLDS, Lewis - b IN 21 Dec 1843; s David and Jemima Reynolds; 15 Apr 1865 m Susannah Baldwin; during CW serv Co. F, 16th Ind. Inf.; was a school tchr; mbr Oak Ridge MM; d 16 Aug 1917 (1,2,10,29,42,46,50,56,58,59)

RICHARDSON, Norman B. - b 18 Jun 1876; s F.M. and E.

Richardson; d 19 Aug 1881 (29)

ROBBINS, Elmer - b 13 Feb 1879; s Henry C. and Mary (Thomas) Robbins; mbr Pipe Creek MM; d 7 Aug 1879 (1,29)

ROBBINS, Henry C. - b Grant Co. 18 Jun 1840; s Jacob and Lydia Robbins; 24 Apr 1861 m Mary Thomas in Mississinewa Friends MH; mbr Marion MM; d 11 Jun 1895 (1,12,29,46,50, 54,62)

ROBBINS, Mary (Thomas) - b 25 Apr 1844; dt Jeremiah and Elizabeth (Hollingsworth) Thomas; 24 Apr 1861 m Henry Robbins in Mississinewa Friends MH; mbr Marion MM; d 15 Mar 1915 (1,29,38,46,50,53,58,62)

ROMINE, Blanch - b 1883; dt Newton and Della (Hollingsworth) Romine; d Jul 1884 (11,29)

ROMINE, Della (Hollingsworth) - b 5 Jan 1864; dt Isaac and Emily (Thomas) Hollingsworth; m Newton Romine 14 Apr 1883; mbr Mississinewa MM; d 19 Jan 1885 (1,11,16,29,46,65)

SACHSE, Emma E. - infant dt M & M William Sachse; d 1 Nov 1915 (29,38,58)

SANDERS, Myrtle - dt John W. (dec) and Nancy A. (Holmes) Sanders; step-dt Luther Diverblies; d 18 Mar 1899 at age 23y (10,13,16,29,38)

SANDERS, Romulus W. - b Guilford Co., NC 25 Jul 1834; s Milton and Serina (Lindsay) Sanders; m Rachel (Presnall) Small 7 Jul 1875; serv in Confederate Army 1862-65; f mbr Deer Creek MM; mbr M.P. Ch.; d 11 Jun 1886 (1,10,23,29)

SCHOOLEY, Emma - b 17 Apr 18__; dt John and Phebe (Jones) Schooley; mbr Mississinewa MM; d 27 Mar 186_ (1,29)

SCHOOLEY, James L. - b 4 Jan 1858; s John and Phebe (Jones)

Schooley; mbr Mississinewa MM; d 22 Jan 1861 (1,29)

SCHOOLEY, John - b 6 Aug 1815; s Samuel and Rachel (Johnson) Schooley; ca Nov 1841 m Phebe Jones; mbr Mississinewa MM; d 13 Apr 1865 (1,29,30,65)

SCOTT, Clarinda - b 1848; dt Samuel and Matilda (Redenbaugh) Scott; d Aug 1871 (29,46)

SCOTT, Ione - d ca 5 Sep 1896 (29,38); may be bur Oak Ridge Friends Cem (46)

SCOTT, James C. - b 11 Sep 1846; s Samuel and Matilda (Redenbaugh) Scott; d 3 Jun 1863 (29,46)

SCOTT, Samuel - b 30 Jun 1802; m Matilda Redenbaugh; d 6 Sep 1862 (29,46)

SHERIDAN, Mary A. - b 19 Dec 1853; d 10 Feb 1871 (29)

SHIELDS, Arminta Jane (Wroe) - b VA 6 May 1829; dt Benjamin and Elizabeth (Pagett) Wroe; 5 Dec 1849 m John Shields; mbr Marion MM; d 7 Jun 1909 (1,23,24,25,29,31,38,46, 50,59,65)

SHIELDS, Clarinda E. - b OH 20 May 1851; dt John and Arminta J. (Wroe) Shields; mbr Mississinewa MM; d 19 Jul 1869 (1,23,24,25,46,50,59,65)

SHIELDS, John - b Darke Co., OH 21 Jul 1826; s Preston and Delilah (Fulkerson) Shields; 5 Dec 1849 m Arminta J. Wroe; serv Corp., Co. G, 12th Ind. Inf. during CW; d 23 Apr 1918 (1,7,23,25,29,38,46,50,58,59)

SHIPLEY, James - 16 Nov 1851 m Rachel Ann Lyon; murdered 22 Jan 1857 (10,23,27,29)

SHIPLEY, Rachel Ann (Lyon) - 16 Nov 1851 m James Shipley; d Nov 1854 (10,29)

SHUGART, infant - dt John V. and Carrie (Hathaway) Shugart; b & d 21 Sep 1894 (1,29)

SHUGART, infant - child of Clinton S. and Elizabeth <u>Alice</u> (Krim) Shugart; mbr Oak Ridge MM; d 1894 (1,16,29)

SHUGART, Albert E. - b 24 Nov 1867; s Cornelius and Harriett (Coleman) Shugart; 29 Nov 1888 m Jennie Hathaway; att Fairmount Friends Academy; mbr Oak Ridge MM; d ca 12 Nov 1948 (1,16,24,29,38,46,53,59,64,65)

SHUGART, Ann (Whitson) - b IN 24 Mar 1838; dt Amos and Rebecca (Peele) Whitson; m Isaiah R. Shugart 20 Oct 1859 at Deer Creek Friends MH; mbr Oak Ridge MM; d 16 Oct 1922 (1,25,29,38,46,50,53,59,62)

SHUGART, Anna (Esherman/Eshelman) - b OH 11 Dec 1857; dt Peter and Narcissus (Lockhart) Esherman; 26 Sep 1872 m Constantine L. Shugart; mbr Deer Creek MM; d ca 25 Dec 1935 (1,10,29,39,46,50,59)

SHUGART, Bennett L. - b IN 29 Aug 1854; s Cornelius and Harriett (Coleman) Shugart; 24 Feb 1877 m Gulie E. Jay; mbr Fairmount MM; d ca 1 Oct 1946 (1,7,24,25,29,38,46,50,53,59, 64,65)

SHUGART, C.L. - d ca 3 Apr 1895 (29,38)

SHUGART, Carrie (Hathaway) - b Fairmount Twp. 2 Mar 1876; dt John and Mary (Hall) Hathaway; 1 Dec 1891 m John V. Shugart; mbr Oak Ridge MM; d ca 25 Apr 1944 (1,25,29,38, 59,73)

SHUGART, Clinton S. - b Cherokee Co., KS 23 Oct 1867; s Isaiah R. and Ann (Whitson) Shugart; 30 Mar 1893 m Elizabeth <u>Alice</u> Krim; mbr Oak Ridge MM; d ca 11 Mar 1954 (1,16, 29,38,46)

SHUGART, Cornelius - b Wayne Co. 9 Feb 1820; s John and

Sarah (Ratliff) Shugart; 25 Oct 1848 m Harriet T. Coleman; f mbr Deer Creek Anti-slavery MM; mbr Deer Creek MM; 1869, Recorded Friends Minister; f mbr Ind. State Legislature; d 1 Jul 1884 (1,7,11,22,24,25,27,29,46,50,53,54,59,61,62)

SHUGART, Cynthia Anna (Brewer) - b Clinton Co., OH; dt Randall Brewer; 9 Sep 1888 m Henry M. Shugart as his 2nd wife; mbr WCTU; mbr Marion MM; d ca 27 Dec 1935 (1,16,29, 38,46,57,59)

SHUGART, Earl - b 26 Oct 1880; s Henry M. and Martha J. (Winslow) Shugart; mbr Deer Creek MM; d 1 May 1884 (1,10, 29,46,59)

SHUGART, Edith C. - b 18 Nov 1887; dt Bennett L. and Gulie E. (Jay) Shugart; mbr Fairmount MM; d 29 Mar 1933 (1,29,38, 40,44,46,53)

SHUGART, Elizabeth Alice (Krim/Krinn) - b Hocking Co., __ 9 Sep 1867; dt Daniel and Ellen (Sliger) Krim; m Clinton S. Shugart 30 Mar 1893; mbr Oak Ridge MM; d ca 12 Jan 1941 (1,16,29,38,46)

SHUGART, Emma - b 1884; d 1918 (29)

SHUGART, Erasmus C. - b 4 Mar 1860; s John and Rebecca (Guyer) Shugart; m Julia Stafford; f mbr Deer Creek MM; d 27 Apr 1892 (1,11,29,41,46,47,53,59,61,64,65,73)

SHUGART, Gulie E. (Jay) - b IN 3 Dec 1859; dt Dennis and Anna (Coggeshall) Jay; 24 Feb 1877 m Bennett L. Shugart; mbr WCTU; mbr Fairmount MM; d ca 21 Jan 1949 (1,25,29,38, 44,46,50,53,59,64)

SHUGART, Harriet T. (Coleman) - b Wayne Co. 18 Dec 1823; dt Elias and Sarah (Peelle) Coleman; 25 Oct 1848 m Cornelius Shugart; f mbr Deer Creek Anti-slavery MM; mbr Deer Creek MM; d 27 Jul 1886 (1,24,25,29,46,49,50,53,59,64,65)

SHUGART, Henry M. - b Grant Co. 16 Sep 1846; s George and Abigail (Osborn) Shugart; 1st m Martha J. Winslow 14 Dec 1871; 2nd m Cynthia Anna Brewer 9 Sep 1888; mbr Deer Creek MM; d 6 Feb 1920 (1,7,10,16,29,38,42,44,46,50,57,58,59 64,65)

SHUGART, Isaiah R. - b Grant Co. 16 Nov 1836; s John and Sarah (Ratliff) Shugart; m Ann Whitson 20 Oct 1859 at Deer Creek Friends MH; f mbr Oak Ridge MM; Recorded Friends Minister; d 21 Jun 1891 (1,7,11,27,29,41,46,50,53,59,62,73)

SHUGART, Jennie (Hathaway) - b 13 Mar 1869; dt John and Mary (Hall) Hathaway; 28 Nov 1888 m Albert E. Shugart; mbr Oak Ridge MM; d ca 12 May 1958 (1,24,29,38,46,59)

SHUGART, John J. - b Wayne Co. 5 Sep 1827; s John and Sarah (Ratliff) Shugart; m Rebecca Guyer 21 Dec 1847; mbr Marion MM; d 1 Apr 1910 (1,7,25,29,31,38,46,53,59,64,65,73)

SHUGART, John V. - b Grant Co. 29 Sep 1866; s John and Rebecca (Guyer) Shugart; Miami Co., 1st m Mildred L. Canaday ca 1888; 2nd m Carrie Hathaway 1 Dec 1891; mbr South Marion MM; d 24 Jun 1942 (1,25,29,31,46,57,59,64,65,73)

SHUGART, Lorenzo L. - b 5 Aug 1860; s Isaiah R. and Ann (Whitson) Shugart; mbr Oak Ridge MM; d 8 Apr 1892 (1,29,46)

SHUGART, Mabel - b 12 Jun 1891; dt Albert E. and Jennie (Hathaway) Shugart; mbr Oak Ridge MM; d 29 Mar 1919 (1,24,29,38,42,46,58,59)

SHUGART, Martha J. (Winslow) - b NC 30 May 1852; dt Jonathan P. and Jane (Henley) Winslow; 14 Dec 1871 m Henry M. Shugart; mbr & Elder, Deer Creek MM; d 18 Oct 1887 (1,10,29,46,50,59,61,64)

SHUGART, Mary Anna (Thomas) - b IN 11 Jan 1829; dt Jesse and Hannah (Cox) Thomas; 1st m Isaac R. Smith 20 Sep 1848 at Mississinewa Friends MH; m 2nd George Shugart 18 Jun 1873; mbr Marion MM; d 30 Apr 1906 (1,19,24,29,38,46,50,53, 59,62)

SHUGART, Mildred L. (Canaday) - b 2 Sep 1867; dt Thomas Elwood and Sarah Canaday; ca 1888 m John V. Shugart; mbr Deer Creek MM; d 24 Jun 1889 (1,11,25,29,46,59)

SHUGART, Minnie - b 30 Sep 1895; dt John V. and Carrie (Hathaway) Shugart; mbr Deer Creek MM; d 7 Aug 1897 (1,12, 29,38,59)

SHUGART, Myrtle - b 1882; d 1926 (29)

SHUGART, Pearl J. - b 31 Nov 1892; s Henry M. and Cynthia Anna (Brewer) Shugart; f mbr Deer Creek MM; d 25 Dec 1950 (1,29,38,40,46,57,59)

SHUGART, Rebecca (Guyer) - b Wayne Co. 13 Sep 1825; dt Samuel and Rachel (Small) Guyer; Miami Co., 21 Dec 1847 m John Shugart; mbr Deer Creek MM; d 22 Apr 1886 (1,11,25,29, 46,61,64,65,73)

SHUGART, Thurlow Weed - b 19 Jul 1885; s Bennett L. and Gulie E. (Jay) Shugart; grad Fairmount Friends Academy; grad Earlham Coll; mbr Oak Ridge MM; 1915, Recorded Friends Minister; d 21 Mar 1918 (1,25,29,38,42,44,46,53,58,59)

SHUGART, William I. - att Jonesboro Public Sch; d 15 Mar 1882, bur beside his father (11)

SHULL, Myrtle M. - b 10 May 1894; dt George M. and Elnora A. Shull; d 1 Oct 1912 (29,38)

SIMONS, Disa Belle (Boussun) - b Cass Co. 27 May 1869; dt John and Annie Boussan; 22 Sep 1886 m William J. Simons; mbr Back Creek MM; d ca 16 Aug 1957 (1,16,29,38)

SIMONS, Verne A. - b 1902; s William J. and Disa Belle

(Boussun) Simons; f mbr Back Creek MM; d Mar 1988 (1,29)

SIMONS, William J. - b Cass Co. 18 Mar 1860; s Abraham and Malinda J. Simons; m Disa Boussun 22 Sep 1886; mbr Back Creek MM; d ca 10 Mar 1925 (1,7,16,29,38)

SLIGER, Jacob - (29)

SLIGER, Jasper - (29)

SLIGER, Sarah Emma (Green) - b 17 Aug 1863; dt Joseph and Jane (Symons) Green; m John M. Sliger 16 Nov 1882; mbr Mississinewa MM; d 1 Aug 1883 (1,16,29,65)

SMALL, Aaron - b IN 29 Jan 1851; s Josiah and Nancy J. (Boxell) Small; 8 Mar 1874 m Nancy J. Cox; mbr Deer Creek MM; d Fairmount 4 Jul 1902 (1,10,14,29,38,46,47,50,56,59)

SMALL, Alfred H. - b 14 Apr 1856; s Josiah and Nancy J. (Boxell) Small; d 10 Aug 1874 (10,29,46,50)

SMALL, Anna J. - b 5 Feb 1846; dt Jesse and Millicent (Ratliff) Small; mbr Mississinewa MM; d 3 Oct 1855 (1,29,46,65)

SMALL, Clarkey - b 26 Jan 1836; dt Joshua and Jane (Bowen) Small; mbr Mississinewa MM; d Apr 1836 (1,29,46,65)

SMALL, Clarkey - b 26 May 1861; dt Reuben and Elizabeth (Shugart) Small; mbr Mississinewa MM; d 6 Aug 1861 (1,29, 46,60,65)

SMALL, Elizabeth (Draper) - b NC 13 Sep 1793; dt Josiah and Mirium (Newby) Draper; in OH m Jesse Small ca Oct 1813; mbr Mississinewa MM; d Dec 1834 (1,17,29,30,46,65)

SMALL, Elizabeth - b 13 Dec 1825; dt Joshua and Jane (Bowen) Small; mbr Mississinewa MM; d Oct 1829 at age 3y, 10m (1,29,46,65)

SMALL, Elizabeth - b 13 Oct 1831; dt Jesse and Elizabeth (Draper) Small; mbr Mississinewa MM; d 'young' (1,29,46,65)

SMALL, Hannah (Addington) - b 15 Nov 1808; dt Thomas and Mary (Smith) Addington; m Benjamin Small; mbr Baraboo MM, WI; d 13 Jan 1862 (1,9,29,60,62)

SMALL, Jemima (Jones) - b 24 Jun 1811; dt Daniel and Jemima Jones; m 1st __ Cain; 2nd m Jesse Small 24 Aug 1880; mbr Mississinewa MM; d 13 Aug 1885 (1,9,29,61)

SMALL, Jesse - b 25 Dec 1776; s Obadiah and Lydia (Bundy) Small; ca Oct 1813 m Elizabeth Draper in OH; mbr Mississinewa MM; d 3 Jan 1850 (1,7,29,30,46,65)

SMALL, Jesse - b Highland Co., OH 25 Dec 1809; s Joseph and Clarissa 'Clarky' (Perisho) Small; 15 Dec 1836 m Millicent Ratliff at Deer Creek Friends MH; m 2nd Jemima (Jones) Cain 24 Aug 1880; mbr Mississinewa MM; killed by train 21 Jun 1884 (1,9,11,24,25,46,50,54,59,61,65)

SMALL, Joseph R. - b IN 19 Oct 1838; s Jesse and Millicent (Ratliff) Small; 25 Sep 1861 m Sarah Ann Overman at Mississinewa Friends MH; mbr Marion MM; d 10 Dec 1906 (1,7,24 25,29,38,46,50,54,59,62,65)

SMALL, Josiah - b IN 9 Feb 1827; s Jesse and Elizabeth (Draper) Small; m Nancy Jane Boxell 28 Jan 1850; f mbr Mississinewa MM; d 6 Apr 1878 (1,10,11,29,46,50,54,59,65)

SMALL, Millicent (Ratliff) - b IN 5 Feb 1819; dt Joseph and Sarah (Shugart) Ratliff; 15 Dec 1836 m Jesse Small at Deer Creek Friends MH; mbr & Elder, Mississinewa MM; d 9 Jan 1879 (1,8,11,24,25,27,29,46,50,51,53,59,61,65)

SMALL, Milly 'Polly' - b 11 Apr 1811; m Nathan Small; mbr Maple Run MM; d 2 Nov 1871 (25,29,64,65)

SMALL, Nancy Jane (Boxell) - b Belmont Co., OH 28 Nov

1830; dt William and Catherine (Parson) Boxell; m Josiah Small 28 Jan 1850; mbr W.M. Ch.; d 20 Oct 1890 (7,10,11,29,46, 50,53,59)

SMALL, Perley E. - b 4 Apr 1879; s Samuel I. and Sarah J. (Price) Small; d 7 Apr 1879 (10,29)

SMALL, Rachel - b IN 3 Nov 1843; dt Reuben and Elizabeth (Shugart) Small; mbr Back Creek MM; d 31 Jul 1861 (1,29,46, 50,60,62)

SMALL, Rebecca - b Sep 1862; dt Reuben and Elizabeth (Shugart) Small; mbr Mississinewa MM; d 26 Sep 1862 (1,29,46)

SMALL, Roxie Ann - dt Winton D. and Mary J. (Albright) Small; b & d 5 Mar 1940 (29,38,46)

SMALL, Russell - b 28 May 1886; s William and Melissa (Smith) Small; d 24 Jun 1892 (11,16,29)

SMALL, Sarah Ann - b 1 Sep 1824; dt Amos and Rachel (Hiatt) Small; mbr Mississinewa MM; d 10 Jan 1831 (1,29, 46,65)

SMALL, Sarah Ann (Overman) - b IN 11 Nov 1842; dt Joel and Mary (Smith) Overman; 25 Sep 1861 m Joseph R. Small at Mississinewa Friends MH; mbr Marion MM; d ca 24 Jan 1929 (1,24,25,29,38,46,50,59,62,65)

SMALL, Silas O. - b IN 10 Feb 1853; s Jesse and Millicent (Ratliff) Small; mbr Mississinewa MM; d 8 Mar 1875 (1,29,46, 50,59,61,65)

SMALL, Viola - b 22 May 1864; dt Joseph R. and Sarah Ann (Overman) Small; mbr Marion MM; d ca 9 Oct 1951 (1,25,29, 38,46,59,65)

SMITH, Allen J. - b IN 18 Mar 1853; s Isaac R. and Mary (Thomas) Smith; m Margaret E. Canaday prior to Apr 1882;

mbr Marion MM; d 29 May 1915 (1,7,24,29,38,46,50,58,59,65)

SMITH, Amanda - b IN 14 Jan 1858; dt Isaac R. and Mary (Thomas) Smith; mbr Mississinewa MM; d 4 Nov 1867 (1,29, 46,50,65)

SMITH, Ann (Randall) - b SC 15 Jan 1797; dt Isaac and Sarah Randall; m Jonathan Smith prior to 19 Jul 1834; mbr Mississinewa MM; d 13 Nov 1872 (1,29,30,50,54,65)

SMITH, Dollie - dt John J. and M.L. Smith; d 29 Apr 1895 at age 6y (12,29,38)

SMITH, Druzilla - b 11 May 1853; dt George W. and Elizabeth (Murray) Smith; d 1 Jul 1853 (10,29)

SMITH, Everett - s Allen J. and Margaret E. (Canaday) Smith; mbr Mississinewa MM; d 20 Dec 1884 at age 15m (29,61)

SMITH, Isaac R. - b OH 16 Jan 1828; s Jesse and Martha (Randall) Smith; 20 Sep 1848 at Mississinewa Friends MH m Mary Thomas; mbr Mississinewa MM; d 19 Apr 1871 (1,24,25,29,30, 46,50,54,59,62,65)

SMITH, Jesse - b SC 5 Jun 1791; m Martha Randall 11 Apr 1820; 1841 came to Grant Co. from Preble Co., OH; mbr Mississinewa MM; d 2 Jan 1871 (1,23,29,30,46,50,54,65)

SMITH, Josephine - dt Allen J. and Margaret E. (Canaday) Smith; mbr Amboy MM; d 21 Aug 1899 (1,29,38,46)

SMITH, Leander - b 25 Jul 1849; s Isaac R. and Mary (Thomas) Smith; mbr Mississinewa MM; d 16 Aug 1849 (1,29,46,65)

SMITH, Margaret 'Maggie' E. (Canaday) - b Miami Co. 7 Feb 1863; dt Oliver H. and Martha (Stanley) Canaday; m Allen J. Smith prior to Apr 1882; mbr Marion MM; d ca 17 Feb 1959 (1,38,46,59)

SMITH, Martha (Randall) - b SC 23 Jul 1795; dt Isaac and
Sarah Randall; 11 Apr 1820 m Jesse Smith; mbr Mississinewa
MM; d 3 Dec 1863 (1,23,29,30,45,46,50,65)

SMITH, Milia 'Milly' (Morris) - b 9 Dec 1839; dt Nathan and
Miriam Morris; at Back Creek Friends MH 25 Nov 1858 m
Thomas B. Smith; mbr Back Creek MM; d 18 Mar 1859 (1,29)

SMITH, Minnie Maria (Yates) - b 1890; dt William and
Nancy Yates; 26 Sep 1914 m Morton Smith; f mbr Marion
MM; d 1981 (1,29,35)

SMITH, Morton - b 1887; 26 Sep 1914 m Minnie Maria Yates;
d ca 24 Aug 1941 (1,29,35,38)

SMITH, Rachel (Overman) - b OH 13 Sep 1826; dt Eli and
Polly (Thomas) Overman; 21 Sep 1842 m Ephraim Smith in
Mississinewa Friends MH; mbr Mississinewa MM; d 26 Oct
1859 (1,24,25,29,46,59,60,62,65)

SMITH, Rebecca (Jones) - b 5 Mar 1831; dt Daniel and
Elizabeth (Small) Jones; m William I. Smith 19 Sep 1849;
mbr Mississinewa MM; d 5 Nov 1854 (1,29,65)

SMITH, Sarah - b 1866; dt Francis M. and Corintha E.
(Skinner) Smith; d 1908 (10,29)

SMITH, Viola (Trowbridge) - b 20 May 1858; 5 Oct 1892 m
Milo Smith as his 2nd wife; d 12 May 1902 (14,16,29,38,46)

SMITH, William I. - b Preble Co., OH 13 Dec 1830; s Jesse and
Martha (Crandall) Smith; 1st m Rebecca Jones 19 Sep 1849;
2nd m Catharine Howell; mbr Marion MM; d 1910 (1,29,65)

STAFFORD, Mary K. - b 19 Jul 1853; dt J. and S.L. Stafford; d
12 Sep 1854 (29)

STAFFORD, Matilda - b 11 Aug 1859; dt J. and L. Stafford; d 2
May 1860 (29)

STALLINGS, Melissa Ellen - b IN 2 Jan 1858; dt Robert R. and Mary (Pearson) Stallings; mbr Mississinewa MM; d 21 May 1878 (1,29,50,61,65)

STALLINGS, Mary (Pearson) - b Randolph Co. 14 Dec 1834; dt Joseph and Sarah (Johnson) Pearson; m Robert R. Stallings 18 Aug 1855; mbr Marion MM; d 17 Jan 1909, funeral in South Marion Friends MH (1,8,29,31,38,50,59,65)

STALLINGS, Robert R. - b VA 10 Dec 1832; m Mary Pearson 18 Aug 1855; mbr Marion MM; d ca 12 Jun 1913 (1,7,8,29,31,32, 38,50,54,59,65)

STALLINGS, Walter L. - b 12 Sep 1887; s Joseph Pearson and Sarah (Evans) Stallings; may be mbr Marion MM; d 27 Jun 1891 (1,29,47)

STEPHENS, Elias Robert - b Fairfield, OH 1790; s John Stephens; serv as soldier during War of 1812; mbr Methodist Ch.; d 1 Oct 1876 (24,29)

STEPHENS, Erma - b 30 Jun 1901; child of A.C. and A.E. Stephens; d 16 Jul 1901 (29)

STEPHENS, Lucy B. (Small) - b 27 Apr 1866; dt Josiah and Nancy J. (Boxell) Small; 13 Apr 1884 m Benoni H. Stephens; d 27 Sep 1892 (16,29,46,47)

STOTLER/STOTTER, Mattias - b VA 11 Jan 1810; m Rebecca; drowned in Mississinewa River 5 Jun 1862 (23,27,29,50)

STOUT, Sarah Ann (Shugart) - b 20 Aug 1857; dt John and Rebecca (Guyer) Shugart; m 1st Jesse Edgerton 10 Oct 1878; m 2nd William E. Stout 20 Aug 1909; mbr Marion MM; d ca 26 Jul 1934 at age 76 (1,10,15,29,38,40,59)

THOMAS, infant - (29)

THOMAS, infant - child of Eli Thomas; d ca 21 Sep 1900

(29,38,46)

THOMAS, infant - child of Hubert L. and Mary E. (Modlin) Thomas; mbr Oak Ridge MM; d ca 11 Nov 1910 (1,16,29,46)

THOMAS, Anna (Schooley) - b Wayne Co. 26 Apr 1828; dt Isaac and Celia (Thomas) Schooley; 21 Oct 1846 at Mississinewa Friends MH m Eli Thomas as his 1st wife; mbr Mississinewa MM; d 26 Jan 1853 (1,24,25,29,46,59,65)

THOMAS, Anna Jane (Leverton) - b 2 Feb 1845; dt Charles and Margaret Leverton; 10 Aug 1865 m Elwood Thomas; mbr Marion MM; d 5 Dec 1903 (1,10,14,29,33,38,46,47,59,65)

THOMAS, Anna Nancy - b 1875; d ca 6 Nov 1975 (29,38)

THOMAS, C. Marie - b 1899; m C. William Thomas (29)

THOMAS, Calvin - b 10 Jun 1847; s William and Mary Martha (Addington) Thomas; mbr Mississinewa MM; d 12 Jun 1847 (1,29,46,65)

THOMAS, Caroline 'Carrie' W. (Lacey) - b IN 8 Nov 1852; dt James and Elizabeth Lacey; 11 Jan 1872 m Isaac Thomas; f mbr Deer Creek MM; d 18 Jun 1943 (1,10,29,38,46,50,59)

THOMAS, Charles William - b 1901; d Apr 1975 (29)

THOMAS, Claribel - b 18 Aug 1868; dt H. and E.R. Thomas; d 19 Sep 1868 (29)

THOMAS, Clarkson - b 15 Aug 1855; s Noah and Elizabeth (Overman) Thomas; mbr Mississinewa MM; d 17 Jan 1857 (1,29,46,60,65)

THOMAS, Clifford - b Feb 1905; s Lester C. and Elsie E. (Jackson) Thomas; d ca 2 Aug 1905 (15,19,29,38,46)

THOMAS, Daniel - b 3 Aug 1844; s Enoch and Jane (Votaw)

Thomas; mbr Mississinewa MM; d 22 Aug 1844 (1,29,46,65)

THOMAS, David - b IN 13 Dec 1849; s Henry and Lydia (Elliott) Thomas; 20 Aug 1880 m 1st Sarah J. Small; 2nd m Ida May; mbr Pipe Creek MM; d 10 Mar 1925 (1,7,29,38,46, 50,58)

THOMAS, Eli - b Randolph Co. 31 Aug 1825; s Jesse and Hannah (Cox) Thomas; 21 Oct 1846 m Anna Schooley in Mississinewa Friends MH; 2nd m Melissa Willcutts 23 Apr 1854; 3rd m Minerva M. Thomas 8 Dec 1877; mbr Marion MM; d 15 Jan 1918 (1,7,10,24,25,27,29,38,42,46,50,53,54,58,59,65)

THOMAS, Eli C. - b 9 Mar 1884; s Sylvanus C. and Mary R. (Knight) Thomas; d 6 Jun 1888 (1,10,11,29,46)

THOMAS, Eli R. - b 20 Oct 1869; s Robert C. and Sarah (Modlin) Thomas; Feb 1887 m Alvina Hockett; mbr Amboy MM; d Lawton, Pulaski Co. 24 Feb 1904 (1,14,29,38,46)

THOMAS, Elizabeth 'Betsey' (Overman) - b Wayne Co. 1 Jun 1820; dt Ephraim and Miriam (Draper) Overman; 14 Dec 1836 m Noah Thomas; mbr Mississinewa MM; d 23 Dec 1892 (1,29, 46,50,53,55,59,65)

Thomas, Elizabeth (Hollingsworth) - b OH 25 Nov 1824; dt Isaac and Jane (Coppock) Hollingsworth; 20 May 1840 m Jeremiah Thomas at Mississinewa Friends MH; mbr Mississinewa MM; d 18 Feb 1879 (1,7,29,46,50,53,65)

THOMAS, Elma (Stout) - b Orange Co. 1 Jun 1849; dt Silas and Martha (King) Stout; 17 Apr 1872 m John Q. Thomas; mbr Marion MM; d ca 26 Oct 1914 (1,23,29,38,46,50,58,59)

THOMAS, Elsie E. (Jackson) - b May 1882; m Lester C. Thomas; d 1 May 1929 (15,29,38,58)

THOMAS, Elwood - b 25 Jan 1841; s Noah and Elizabeth (Overman) Thomas; mbr Mississinewa MM; d 27 May 1841

(1,29,46,65)

THOMAS, Elwood - b IN 11 Jun 1844; s Jeremiah and Elizabeth (Hollingsworth) Thomas; 10 Aug 1865 m Anna Jane
Leverton; mbr Marion MM; d 11 Jul 1919 (1,7,29,38,46,50,53,
54,58,59,65,73)

THOMAS, Emma M. (Southworth) - dt William and Sarah
C. Southworth; 15 Sep 1903 m Charles C. Thomas; d 29 Sep
1918 (15,29,38,58,59)

THOMAS, Enoch - b IN 20 Jul 1846; s Jeremiah and Elizabeth
(Hollingsworth) Thomas; mbr Mississinewa MM; d 19 Dec
1874 (1,29,46,50,53,65)

THOMAS, Frank M. - b 1914; d 1978 (29)

THOMAS, Glenn - b 4 Mar 1875; s Sylvanus C. and Mary R.
(Knight) Thomas; f mbr Mississinewa MM; d 26 Jul 1892
(1,10,11,29,46,65,73)

THOMAS, Guy - b 10 May 1877; s Sylvanus C. and Mary R.
(Knight) Thomas; f mbr Mississinewa MM; d 15 Mar 1911
(1,10,29,32,38,46,65)

THOMAS, Hannah (Cox) - b NC 15 Aug 1798; dt Jeremiah
and Margery (Piggott) Cox; in Whitewater Friends MH 3
Nov 1819 m Jesse Thomas; mbr Mississinewa MM; d 30 Aug
1868 (1,8,24,25,29,46,50,53,59,65,71)

THOMAS, Hannah L. - b 3/11 Nov 1855; dt Enoch and Jane
(Votaw) Thomas; mbr Mississinewa MM; d 28 Sep 1856 (1,29,
46,65)

THOMAS, Harrison 'Harry' - b 1889; s Isaac and Caroline
(Lacey) Thomas; f mbr Deer Creek MM; d ca 15 Jan 1908 (1,29,
31,38,46)

THOMAS, Hubert L. - b 27 Mar 1869; s Elwood and Anna

(Leverton) Thomas; m Mary Elizabeth Modlin 24 Jun 1893; mbr South Marion MM; d ca 14 Apr 1937 (1,7,16,29,38,46)

THOMAS, Ida M. (Thomas?) - b 1860; dt Reuben and Amanda P___; m David Thomas; f mbr Pipe Creek MM; mbr Christian Ch., Converse; d ca 24 Jan 1936 (1,29,38)

THOMAS, Isaac - b IN 8 Mar 1848; s Jeremiah and Elizabeth (Hollingsworth) Thomas; 11 Jan 1872 m Caroline Lacey; f mbr Deer Creek MM; d 31 Oct 1917 (1,10.29,38,46,50,53,54,58, 59,65)

THOMAS, Jehiel - b 12 Jan 1853; s Eli and Anna (Schooley) Thomas; mbr Mississinewa MM; d 1 Feb 1853 (1,29,46,65)

THOMAS, Jennie (Sirk) - b 1878; m Oliver J. Thomas 17 Nov 1892; d 1960 (16,29)

THOMAS, Jeremiah - b IN 19 Aug 1820; s Jesse and Hannah (Cox) Thomas; 20 May 1840 m Elizabeth Hollingsworth in Mississinewa Friends MH; mbr Mississinewa MM; d 24 Mar 1874 (1,24,25,29,46,50,53,54,59,65)

THOMAS, Jesse - b SC 9 Sep 1796; s John and Lydia (Snead) Thomas; in Whitewater Friends MH 3 Nov 1819 m Hannah Cox; mbr & Elder, Mississinewa MM; d 31 Mar 1859 (1,9,24,25, 29,46,53,59,60,62,65)

THOMAS, Jesse - b 9 Oct 1835; s Jesse and Hannah (Cox) Thomas; mbr Mississinewa MM; d 5 Mar 1836 (1,65)

THOMAS, Jesse - b 17 Oct 1844; s William and Mary Martha (Addington) Thomas; mbr Mississinewa MM; d 9 Nov 1845 (1,29,46,65)

THOMAS, Jesse J. - b IN 8 Mar 1850; s Jeremiah and Elizabeth (Hollingsworth) Thomas; was a prominent tchr; f mbr Mississinewa MM; d 20 Dec 1894, funeral in South Marion Friends MH (1,11,29,46,47,50,53,65)

THOMAS, John Q. - b Grant Co. 6 Jan 1847; s Milton and Martha (Way) Thomas; 17 Apr 1872 m Elma Stout; 2nd m Irene Harmon 10 Oct 1917; serv Co. D, 42nd Ind. Inf. during CW; mbr Marion MM; d 18 Apr 1926 (1,7,29,35,38,44,46,50,54, 58,59)

THOMAS, John Benton - b 27 Apr 1914; s M & M Leonard Thomas; d 8 Aug 1921 (29,38,58,59)

THOMAS, Kenneth V. - b 2 May 1891; s Sylvanus C. and Mary R. (Knight) Thomas; d 17 Apr 1899, funeral in South Marion Friends MH (1,10,13,29,38,46,47)

THOMAS, Lester Charles - b 2 Feb 1881; s Elwood and Anna Jane (Leverton) Thomas; m Elsie E. Jackson; mbr Marion MM; d Anderson ca 19 Sep 1936 (1,15,29,38,30,46,59)

THOMAS, Lillian - b & d 1860; dt Robert C. and Sarah (Modlin) Thomas (46)

THOMAS, Loren - b 5 Nov 1881; s David and Sarah J. (Small) Thomas; d 23 Dec 1881 (10,29,46)

THOMAS, Marcus M. - b Grant Co. 27 Oct 1850; s Eli and Anna (Schooley) Thomas; m Sarah Elizabeth Shugart 26 Oct 1871; f mbr Deer Creek MM; Recorded Friends Minister; d ca 18 Jul 1937 (1,10,24,25,29,38,46,50,59,64,65)

THOMAS, Mary Elizabeth (Modlin) - b 13 Jul 1871; dt Nathan P. and Luella J. (Gardner) Modlin; m Hubert L. Thomas 24 Jun 1893; mbr South Marion MM; d ca 26 Jun 1952 (1,16,29, 38,46)

THOMAS, Mary Martha (Addington) - b OH 2 Nov 1822; dt Henry Addington; 6 Jun 1839 m William Thomas; mbr Mississinewa MM; d 28 Jul 1861 (1,10,29,46,50,59,60,62,65)

THOMAS, Melissa 'Milly' (Wilcutts) - b IN 16 May 1825; dt Clark and Eunice (Hall) Wilcutts; 23 Apr 1854 m Eli Thomas

as his 2nd wife; mbr & Overseer, Mississinewa MM; d 22 Sep
1876 (1,10,24,25,29,46,50,59,61,65)

THOMAS, Mildred - b 1904; dt John C. and Gracie (Moore)
Thomas; d ca 15 Aug 1907 (15,19,29,38,46)

THOMAS, Milton - b SC 6 Jul 1811; s Elijah and Susannah
(Snead) Thomas; m Martha Way 15 Jul 1837; f mbr Mississinewa MM; d 14 Apr 1879 (1,10,17,23,29,46,50,54,55,59)

THOMAS, Minerva M. (Thomas) - b 30 Nov 1840; dt Milton
and Martha (Way) Thomas; 8 Dec 1877 m Eli Thomas as his
3rd wife; mbr Marion MM; d 18 Dec 1928 (1,10,24,25,29,38,46,
53,58,59)

THOMAS, Nathan - b 23 Sep 1832; s Jesse and Hannah (Cox)
Thomas; mbr Mississinewa MM; d 6 Feb 1833 (1,65)

THOMAS, Noah - b Wayne Co. 10 May 1818; s John and
Lydia (Snead) Thomas; 1830 came to Grant Co.; at Mississin-
ewa Friends MH 14 Dec 1836 m Elizabeth Overman; mbr
Mississinewa MM; d 23 Dec 1892 (1,23,29,46,47,50,53,55,59,65)

THOMAS, Noah J. - d ca 23 Dec 1935 (29,38); prob b IN 4 Feb
1842; s Jesse and Hannah (Cox) Thomas; 23 Aug 1861 m
Penina Jane Modlin; mbr Marion MM (1,10,24,46,50,53,65)

THOMAS, Oliver J. - b 13 Nov 1871; s Elwood and Anna Jane
(Leverton) Thomas; 1st m June Ward; 2nd m Jennie Sirk 17
Nov 1892; mbr Marion MM; d 24 Nov 1919 (1,7,16,29,38,46,
58,59)

THOMAS, Rachel (Way) - b NC 22 Oct 1804; dt Joseph and
Sarah (Ozbun) Way; at Center Friends MH, Wayne Co., 23
May 1822 m Daniel Thomas; f mbr Deer Creek Anti-slavery
MM; d 27 Jan 1864 (1,8,9,17,29,55,68,69)

THOMAS, Rhoda J. - b IN 30 May 1857; dt Jeremiah and
Elizabeth (Hollingsworth) Thomas; mbr Mississinewa MM;

d 22 Dec 1874 (1,29,46,50,65)

THOMAS, Robert C. - b IN 25 Apr 1837; s Jesse and Hannah (Cox) Thomas; m Sarah Modlin 15 Oct 1857; mbr Pipe Creek MM; d 7 Aug 1880 (1,7,10,24,25,29,46,50,53,59,65)

THOMAS, Sarah (Modlin) - b IN 10 Aug 1836; dt Reuben and Nancy (Harlen) Modlin; m Robert C. Thomas 15 Oct 1857; mbr Pipe Creek MM; d 5 Jun 1889 (1,10,29,46,50,59)

THOMAS, Sarah Ann (Smith) - b OH 5 Jan 1840; dt Jonathan and Ann (Randall) Smith; 23 Sep 1853 m Henry Thomas; mbr Mississinewa MM; d 24 Apr 1861 (1,29,46,50,60,62,65)

THOMAS, Sarah Elizabeth (Shugart) - b IN 9 Aug 1855; dt Henry and Nancy (Lomax) Shugart; m Marcus L. Thomas 26 Oct 1871; mbr Deer Creek MM; d ca 16 May 1920 (1,10,24,29,38, 46,50,58,59,64)

THOMAS, Sarah Jane (Small) - b IN 8 Jan 1856; dt Jesse and Millicent (Ratliff) Small; m David Thomas 26 Aug 1880; mbr Mississinewa MM; d 30 Apr 1882 (1,10,11,29,46,50,61,65)

THOMAS, Sherman S. - b 14 Oct 1866; s Elwood and Anna Jane (Leverton) Thomas; mbr Deer Creek MM; d 20 Jul 1888, funeral in South Marion Friends MH (1,11,29,46,47,61,65)

THOMAS, Sylvanus - b 24 Sep 1845; s Enoch and Jane (Votaw) Thomas; mbr Mississinewa MM; d 27 Sep 1845 (1,65)

THOMAS, Sylvanus C. - b IN 8 Apr 1848; s Eli and Anna (Schooley) Thomas; m Mary R. Knight 20 Sep 1873; f mbr Mississinewa MM; d 25 Nov 1913 (1,10,24,25,29,32,38,46,50,54, 59,65)

THOMAS, Thomas - s Eli and Melissa (Wilcutts) Thomas; b and d 27 Oct 1857 (1,29)

THOMAS, Thomas Clarkson - b IN 27 Nov 1857; s Eli and

Melissa (Wilcutts) Thomas; mbr Mississinewa MM; d 25 Jun 1878 (1,11,24,29,46,50,59,65)

THOMAS, William - b IN 10 May 1818; s John and Lydia (Snead) Thomas; 6 Jun 1839 m Mary Martha Addington; 21 Dec 1865 m Pheraba (Overman) Wilson in Back Creek Friends MH; mbr Pipe Creek MM; d ca 17 Jun 1897, funeral in Marion Friends MH (1,10,12,29,38,46,50,53,55,59,62,65)

THOMAS, William - b 15 Apr 1859; s Noah and Elizabeth (Overman) Thomas; mbr Mississinewa MM; d 18 Apr 1859 (1,29,46,65)

THOMAS, Wilson - b 5 Aug 1844; s Simeon and Esther (Coats) Thomas; mbr Mississinewa MM; d 25 Sep 1844 (1,65)

THOMAS, Zedith M. - b 10 Mar 1893; d 27 Jul 1893 (29)

THOMPSON, infant - child of Samuel Thompson; d ca 22 Jul 1907 (29,38)

THOMPSON, Bessie Olive Eva - dt M & M Samuel Thompson; d 2 Feb 1900 at age 4y (13,29,38,47)

THOMPSON, Cletus O. - s M & M Samuel Thompson; d ca 20 Mar 1909 at age 11da (29,31,38)

THOMPSON, Ruth J. - dt M & M Samuel Thompson; d 19 Oct 1908 at age ca 11y (29,31,38)

THORNBURG, William - d ca 17 Aug 1906 (29,38)

TITUS, George A. - b 1877; d ca 27 Jun 1962 (29,38)

TOWNSEND, Rev. Caldwell G. - b IN 28 Jun 1844; s Eli and Rachel (Moore) Townsend; 23 Sep 1863 m Martha M. Hodgin at Cedar Friends MH; pastor, South Marion Friends Ch.; d 14 Jan 1895, funeral in Marion Friends MH (1,8,12,29,38,50,59)

TOWNSEND, Martha M. (Hodgin) - b 1 Sep 1845; dt Nathan and Mourning (Coffin) Hodgin; 23 Sep 1863 m Caldwell G. Townsend at Cedar Friends MH; mbr Marion MM; d ca 14 Nov 1918 (1,8,29,38,58,59)

TUCKER, Clatie - b 9 Jul 1875; s Julius E. and Sarah E. (Knight) Tucker; d 30 May 1876 (10,29)

TUCKER, Granville - b 28 Feb 1796; d 15 Jun 1882 (29)

TUCKER, Sarah E. (Knight) - b IN 9 Nov 1847; dt James and Rachel (Wilcutts) Knight; m Julius E. Tucker 8 Aug 1874; mbr Deer Creek MM; d 23 Sep 1879 (1,10,29,46,50,65)

VINNEDGE, John W. - b IN 1846; 1st m Eunice Haisley prior to Apr 1871; 2nd m Rebecca Anna Fisher 28 May 1896; mbr Cherry Grove MM; Recorded Friends Minister; d ca 4 Mar 1908 (1,7,8,16,29,38,50)

VINNEDGE, Rebecca Anna (Fisher) - b IN 31 Jul 1854; dt Amos and Ann Fisher; m John W. Vinnedge 28 May 1896; mbr Cherry Grove MM; d 22 Apr 1906 (1,8,16,19,29,38,50)

VOTAW, Ezra S. - b Hamilton Co. 16 Jan 1849; s Jacob and Huldah (Thomas) Votaw; mbr Mississinewa MM; d 13 Oct 1876 (1,29,65)

VOTAW, Huldah (Thomas) - b Wayne Co. 15 Mar 1827; dt Jesse and Hannah (Cox) Thomas; 19 Nov 1845 m Jacob Votaw in Mississinewa MH; mbr Mississinewa MM; d 30 Jul 1853 (1,24,25,29,46,53,59,62,65)

VOTAW, Nathaniel - 30 Mar 1853; s Jacob and Huldah (Thomas) Votaw; mbr Mississinewa MM; d 17 Aug 1853 (1,29,59,65)

WARD, Guy - b 1894; d ca 25 Oct 1894 (29,38)

WARD, M. - (29)

WATKINS, James - d ca 21 Sep 1910 (29,38)

WEESNER, Elizabeth (Wiant) - b 13 Jun 1835; 5 Jan 1858 m
Micajah M. Weesner as his 1st wife; mbr U.B. Ch.; d 17 Apr
1879 (10,11,29)

WEESNER, Elizabeth R. (Myers) - b 24 Jun 1841; 25 Apr 1880
m Micajah M. Weesner as his 2nd wife; d 28 Sep 1925
(10,29,38)

WEESNER, George - child of M & M William Weesner; d ca
7 Oct 1895 at age 3y (12,29,38)

WEESNER, Jane (Thomas) - b IN 14 Mar 1853; dt Jeremiah
and Elizabeth (Hollingsworth) Thomas; 14 Mar 1871 m
David Weesner; mbr Deer Creek MM; d 16 Nov 1874 (1,10,11,
29,46,50,64,65)

WEESNER, Micajah M. - b IN 16 Jul 1838; 1st m Elizabeth
Wiant 5 Jan 1858; 2nd m Elizabeth R. Myers 25 Apr 1880; d 27
Apr 1917 (7,10,29,38,54)

WEESNER, Susannah - d 1865 (29)

WEESNER, William H. - b 1859; d ca 12 Apr 1927 (29,38)

WELCH, Webster G. - b Iredell Co., NC 16 Oct 1804; s Samuel
and Chloe Welch; 1st m Mary Cooper 3 Mar 1831; 2nd m
Mary F.; f mbr Miami MM, OH; mbr Friends; d 13 Jan 1894
(11,18,29,30,71)

WHITE, George Washington - Hawkins Co., TN 24 Dec 1829;
s Drury and Elizabeth White; 1845 came to IN; 27 Dec 1849 m
Hannah J. Green; d 11 May 1885 (10,11,23,27,29,50,53,54)

WHITE, Hannah Jane (Green) - b Randolph Co. 13 Apr 1834;
dt James and Elizabeth Green; 27 Dec 1849 m George W.
White; d 23 Aug 1885 (10,11,23,29,50)

WHITE, Sarah Candace - dt George W. and Hannah J. (Green) White; d Oct 1893, "buried on bank of Mississinewa" (11)

WIAND/WYAND, Delphia - b 5 Mar 1890; dt Harrison and Paulina Ellen (Stalker) Wiand; mbr Deer Creek MM; d 5 Mar 1895 (1,12,29,38)

WIAND, George W. - d ca 4 May 1924 (29,38)

WIAND, Harrison - m Rachel Betty; serv Co. D, 153rd Ind. Inf. during CW; mbr U.B. Ch.; d 27 May 1867 (7,23,24,25,29)

WIAND/WYANT, Harrison - b 22 Feb 1846; s Harrison and Rachel (Betty) Wiant; m Paulina Stalker 24 Nov 1867; mbr Deer Creek MM; d Attica ca 12 Feb 1912 (1,10,25,29,32,38,64)

WIAND, Lewis E. - b IN 15 Aug 1865; d 22 May 1885 (29,54)

WIAND, Mary J. (Compton) - b 21 Mar 1839; 17 Mar 1859 m Israel Wiand as his 1st wife; d 9 Jan 1867 (7,10,29)

WIAND, Paulina (Stalker) - b 2 Feb 1850; dt Thomas and Sara J. (Elliott) Stalker; 24 Nov 1867 m Harrison Wiand; mbr Marion MM; d ca 23 Jan 1923 (1,10,25,29,38,64)

WIAND, Robert - b IN ca 1852; d ca 23 Dec 1919 (29,38,54)

WILLCUTS, infant - child of Albert Willcuts; d 1 May 1896 (29,38)

WILLCUTS, Albert - b IN 3 Jul 1859; s Thomas and Lydia (Mills) Willcuts; m __; mbr Marion MM; d 4 Sep 1896, funeral in South Marion Friends MH (1,12,29,38,50,65)

WILLCUTS, Alfred T. - b 27 Oct 1848; s Jehu and Jerusha (Moore) Willcuts; d 11 Sep 1849 (29,46)

WILLCUTS, Clarkson - b SC 8 Jul 1792; s Thomas and Milly

Willcuts; 1st m __; at Mississinewa Friends MH 2nd m
Eunice Hockett 24 Apr 1839; at Mississinewa Friends MH 3rd
m Sarah (Stratton) Mills 21 Nov 1860; mbr Mississinewa
MM; d 27 Nov 1862 (1,7,17,23,25,29,46,50,53,59,60,62,65)

WILLCUTS, Eunice (Hockett) - b 21 Jun 1802; dt Joseph and
Miriam (Hall) Hockett; at Mississinewa Friends MH 24 Apr
1839 m Clark Willcuts as his 2nd wife; mbr Mississinewa
MM; d 23 Oct 1859 (1,25,29,46,59,60,62,65)

WILLCUTS, Jerusha (Moore) - b 30 Sep 1827; m Jehu Willcuts 2 Dec 1847; d 16 Aug 1850? (10,29,46)

WILLCUTS, Jerusha M. - b 9 Aug 1850; dt Jehu and Jerusha
(Moore) Willcuts; d 27 Aug 1850 (29,46)

WILLCUTS, Pelinia (Baldwin) - b May 1831; 23 Dec 1851 m
John W. Willcuts; d 10 Sep 1852 (10,29)

WILLCUTS, Sarah (Stratton) - b NJ 1 Jan 1804; Warren Co.,
OH 1st m 15 Nov 1821 Curtis Mills (d 18 May 1859); at Mississinewa Friends MH 2nd m Clarkson Willcuts 21 Nov 1860;
mbr Mississinewa MM; d 17 Oct 1884 (1,11,53,61,62,71)

WILLCUTS, Sarah 'Sally' (Morris) - b 20 Jun 1832; dt Caleb
and Mary Morris; 16 Dec 1847 m John Willcuts; d 16 Dec 1849
(10,29,46,53)

WILLIAMS, Elizabeth A. (Burnes) - b Carroll Co. 18 Feb 1844;
dt Charles and Margaret Burnes; 3 Mar 1859 m James Williams; f mbr Mississinewa MM; d 5 May 1915 (1,10,29,38,50)

WILLIAMS, James - b Shelby Co., OH 5 Feb/Apr 1836/1837; s
William and Precocia Williams; m Elizabeth A. Burnes 3
Mar 1859; serv 24th Battalion, Ind. Light Artillery during
CW; f mbr Mississinewa MM; d 6 Sep 1917 (1,10,29,38,50,54)

WILLIAMS, Joseph Marion - b 10 Aug 1862; s James and
Elizabeth A. (Burnes) Williams; d 9 Sep 1878 (10,11,29)

WIMMER, Catherine E. - b Feb 1881; dt Ezekiel R. and Amanda J. (Andrew) Wimmer; d 1 Aug 1881 (10,29)

WIMMER, Virginia - b 25 Dec 1884; dt Ezekiel R. and Amanda J. (Andrew) Wimmer; d 8 Aug 1885 (10,29)

WINSLOW, Ida F. (Davis) - b 1889; dt Oliver S. and Evangeline (Jay) Davis; 28 Mar 1931 m Isaac Clinton Winslow as his 2nd wife; mbr Marion MM; d ca 28 Jan 1957 (1,29,36,38,40,59)

WINSLOW, Isaac Clinton - b 5 Mar 1870; s Aaron and Hannah Ann (Brooks) Winslow; m 1st Laura May Pritchett 23 Apr 1905; m 2nd Ida F. Davis 28 Mar 1931; mbr Back Creek MM; d Mar 1949 (1,15,29,36)

WINSLOW, Jennie M. - b 7 Apr 1892; d 18 May 1921 (29,38)

WINSLOW, Laura May (Pritchett) - b 2 Oct 1878; dt M & M E.J. Pritchett; 23 Apr 1905 m Isaac Clinton Winslow as his 1st wife; d 19 Dec 1905 (15,19,29,56)

WORDEN, Olive Louise - b 1894; d ca 12 Apr 1964 (29,38)

WRIGHT, Joab - b Green Co., TN 19 Jun 1815; s Jesse and Anna (Clearwater) Wright; 1st m Mary Small ca Aug 1837; m 2nd Malinda Elliott 28 Aug 1839; 3rd m Emma Thornburgh 12 Jun 1879; mbr Marion MM; d 3 Dec 1894 (1,7,10,11,24,25,29, 33,50,54,59,65)

WRIGHT, Malinda (Elliott) - b NC 7 Apr 1818; dt Jacob and Ann Elliott; m Joab Wright 28 Aug 1839; Recorded Friends Minister; mbr Mississinewa MM; d 4 May 1878 (1,11,24,29,33, 50,59,65)

WRIGHT, Walter C. - s C.F. and S.L. Wright; b & d 1879 (29)

WYLIE, Peter Curtis - b 1880; d ca 10 Jun 1966 (29,38)

YATES, Nancy Emma (Sheridan) - b Amboy 28 Oct 1858; dt

Abraham and Rachel Sheridan; m William Yates; f mbr
Marion MM; d ca 15 Aug 1913 (1,29,32,38,50)

YATES, William Marion - b IN 16 Jun 1844; s Enoch and
Sarah A. (Edgel) Yates; 1st m Huldah Thomas 20 Sep 1868;
2nd m Nancy Emma Sheridan; f mbr Marion MM; d ca 27 Jul
1914 (1,10,13,29,38,54,58,65)

Deer Creek Friends Cemetery is at the southwest edge
of Marion on the east side of State Road # 9 just south of Old
Kokomo Road. It is located in the NW quarter of the NW
quarter of Section 31, Township 24 N, Range 8 E, Mill
Township, Grant County, Indiana. It includes circa 0.7 acres
and is northeast of the former Deer Creek Friends meetinghouse on the north bank of the beautiful Deer Creek.
Burials no longer occur in this cemetery which is now
owned and cared for by Mill Township.

ALLEN, Martha - b NC 23 Mar 1801; m 1st Lewis Wooton; 16
Oct 1852 m 2nd James Allen; 6 Nov 1830 Recorded Friends
Minister by White River MM; f mbr Deer Creek Anti-slavery
MM; mbr Back Creek MM; d 13 Apr 1863 (1,3,6,8,25,28,49,50,
53,62)

BALDWIN, Daniel - b 4 Jun 1846; s Thomas and Lydia
(Thomas) Baldwin; mbr Mississinewa MM; d 28 Dec 1852 at
Deer Creek Mill (3,21,28,29,45,59,65)

BALDWIN, Ida - b 1 Mar 1861; dt Terah and Isabella (Lucas)
Baldwin; mbr Deer Creek MM; d 7 Sep 1876 (1,3,24,46,59,
64,65)

BALDWIN, Matilda - b 19 Oct 1862; dt Terah and Isabella
(Lucas) Baldwin; d 30 Jul 1863 (3,24,59,64,65); prob bur East
Bethel Cem since grave stone is there (68)

BALDWIN, May - b 22 Oct 1872; dt Terah and Isabella (Lucas)
Baldwin; mbr Deer Creek MM; d 6 Aug 1874 (1,3,24,46,59,64)

BALDWIN, Orange T. - b 16 May 1875; s Terah and Isabella
(Lucas) Baldwin; mbr Deer Creek MM; d 26 Oct 1878 (1,24,
46,59)

BECKET, Mrs. Mary - d Jan 1895 at age 63 (12)

BREWER, James - s William C. and Allie (Owens) Brewer; d
10 Jul 1901 at age 10m (14,47)

BREWER, Allie (Owens) - 13 Aug 1892 m William C.
Brewer; d 3 May 1903 (14,16,47)

CARTER, Rosetta - b 27 Sep 1865; dt Isaac W. and Phebe W.
(Whitson) Carter; mbr Oak Ridge MM; d 5 Feb 1870 (1,25,59)

CARTER, Susan - b 1821; d (3,6,28)

CARTER, Susan Alice - b OH 30 Jun 1855; dt Isaac W. and
Phebe W. (Whitson) Carter; mbr Oak Ridge MM; d 22 Dec
1861 (1,25,46,50,59)

CERTAIN, __ - child of Henry and Charity E. (McCrum)
Certain; d Nov 1898 at age 3 weeks (13)

CERTAIN, Charity/Charlotte E. (McCrum) - m Henry
Certain 6 Sep 1877; d 29 Oct 1898 at age 38 (10,13,47)

CERTAIN, Henry - b IN 13 Aug 1851; s Lewis and Sarah
Certain; 6 Sep 1877 m Charity E. McCrum; d 11 Mar 1906 at
age 54, may be bur in Back Creek Friends Cem (10,19,46,50)

CHARLES, Olive Ann (Jackson) - b 5 Jun 1829; dt Elijah and
Ann (Puckett) Jackson; m Dr. Henry Charles; mbr Mississinewa MM; d 1869 (1,3,6,28,59)

COATS/COATE, Abigail (Shugart) - b 1832; dt John and
Sarah Shugart; sister of George and John Shugart; m Allen
Coate 28 Jun 1850; f mbr Deer Creek Anti-slavery MM; mbr
Back Creek MM; d Dec 1898 (1,3,6,8,10,13,28,49)

COGGESHALL, Lucy - b 20 Apr 1850; dt Nathan and
Gulielma (Shugart) Coggeshall; mbr Mississinewa MM; d 15
Sep 1861 (1,59,60,62,65)

COGGESHALL, Rhoda - b 31 Jul 1856; dt Nathan and
Gulielma (Shugart) Coggeshall; mbr Mississinewa MM; d 25
Dec 1861 (1,59,60,62,65)

COLEMAN, Bennie - b 1830; d 1861 (3,6,28)

COLEMAN, Isadora - b 1794 (3); [may be age 6; dt Bennett B. and Sarah (Shugart) Coleman (25,26)]

COLEMAN, Sally (Peelle) - b NC 21 May 1791; dt Willis and Betsy Peelle; 10 Oct 1820 m Elias Coleman at Conentnea Friends MH, NC; mbr Deer Creek Anti-slavery MM; d 1864 (1,3,6,25,28,49,50,59)

COOK, Mary (Bond) - ca 1867 m Isham/Isom Cook (dec 5 Aug 1869); mbr & Minister Oak Ridge MM; d 19 Apr 1874 at age 29y, 5m, 17da (3,8,33,61)

CRAWLEY, Norma Gail - dt M & M Frank Crawley; d Aug 1906 at age 5y (19)

CRAWLEY, Thomas C. - s M & M Frank Crawley; d Detroit, MI 18 Nov 1928 at age 26, prob bur Deer Creek Friends Cem (58)

CUNNINGHAM, __ - child of James and Lottie (Kelley) Cunningham; d Mar 1896, funeral in Deer Creek Friends MH, may be bur Deer Creek Friends Cem (12,16)

DAVIS, Chloe M. (Harris) - b 22 Mar 1873; dt Newton and Elmina (Bogue) Harris; m Charles W. Davis 3 Sep 1891; mbr Deer Creek MM; d 29 Jun 1899, funeral in Deer Creek Friends MH, prob bur Deer Creek Cem (1,13,16,64)

DAVIS, Wilson - m Elizabeth Tharp 7 Mar 1847; prob f mbr Deer Creek Anti-slavery MM; d May 1897 at age 72 (1,10,-12,59)

DOUGLAS, John - b 1838; d 1849 (3,6,28)

DOUGLAS, Mary - b 1811; d 1849, may be third burial in Deer Creek Friends Cem (3,6,28)

FENSTERMAKER, John - s William Otis and Nellie V. (Harris) Fenstermaker; d 12 Jan 1898 at age 6m, funeral in Deer Creek Friends MH, prob bur Deer Creek Friends Cem (1,13,16,47)

FORESTER, Ruth - infant dt William H. and Emma Florence (Hodson) Forester; d 9 Mar 1916 (1,15,58)

HARRIS, Davis - b 26 Nov 1829; s Thomas and Mary (Shugart) Harris; mbr Deer Creek Anti-slavery MM; d 9 Mar 1851 (1,3,6,28,49,59,65)

HARRIS, Elam - b 2 Apr 1834; s David M. and Rachel (Hunt) Harris; mbr Mississinewa MM; d 31 Jul 1835 (1,65)

HARRIS, George - b 26 Jan 1825; s Thomas and Mary (Shugart) Harris; mbr Mississinewa MM; d 22 Sep 1846, may be second burial in Deer Creek Friends Cem (1,3,6,28,59,65)

HARRIS, Mary (Shugart) - b NC 26 Jan 1798; dt George and Mary (Davis) Shugart; 19 Nov 1818 m Thomas Harris at New Garden MH; f mbr Deer Creek Anti-slavery MM; mbr Mississinewa MM; d 23 Dec 1862 (1,3,6,8,25,28,50,55,59,60,62,64,65)

HARRIS, Rachel (Hunt) - b 15 Oct 1806; dt Abraham and Sarah Hunt; ca Jun 1825 m David M. Harris; mbr Mississinewa MM; d 27 Jul 1836 (1,8,65)

HARRIS, Thomas - b NC 26 Sep 1796; s Obadiah and Maris Harris; 1st m Mary Shugart 19 Nov 1818 at New Garden MH; 2nd m Lydia (Hollingsworth) Jay 25 May 1870 at Center Friends MH; mbr Back Creek MM; was a Medical Dr.; d 5 Oct 1870 (1,3,6,8,25,50,54,55,59,64,65)

HARRIS, Wesley - b 11 May 1846; s Noah and Nancy (Osborn) Harris; mbr Deer Creek Anti-slavery MM; d 25 Oct 1846 (1,3,59)

JACKSON, Andrew - b 1761; may have m Mahala Beales;

mbr Deer Creek Anti-slavery MM; d 1859 (1,3,6,8,28)

JACKSON, Elijah - b NC 1798; m Ann/Rosanna Puckett ca Aug 1817; f mbr Dunkirk Anti-slavery MM; d 1868 (3,6,8,17, 22,28,50)

JOHNSON, Margaret - b 1852?; d 1874 (3)

JOHNSON, Perziler - d 1849 (3)

JOHNSON, Perziler - m; d 15 May 1930 at age 80 (58)

JONES, Lillie E. - b 6 Aug 1873; dt Hiram B. and Mary E. Jones; d 18 Oct 1883 (11); may be bur Mississinewa Friends Cem (29)

JONES, Thomas Clarkson - b IN 5 Nov 1840; s William and Eunice Jones; f mbr Deer Creek Anti-slavery MM; mbr Mississinewa MM; d 9 Feb 1863 at Memphis, TN while serv in Co. C, 89th Ind. Inf. (1,2,3,6,28,50,62)

KELLEY, Xenophus W. - s M & M Henry Kelley; d 26 Apr 1923 (58)

KERLIN, Mary (Small) - b Wayne Co. 15 Sep 1830; dt Amos and Rachel Small; 11 Apr 1850 m Joseph B. Kerlin; mbr Deer Creek MM; d Aug 1879 (1,10,64)

KERSEY, __ - child of Dr. James B. and Eva (Owens) Kersey; d May 1895 at age 6m (12,15)

KERSEY, Eva (Owens) - m James B. Kersey 8 Feb 1893; d Jul 1898, funeral in Back Creek Friends MH (13,16)

LADD, Cicero - b 8 Apr 1855; s Samuel and Charity (Cook) Ladd; mbr Mississinewa MM; d 28 Mar 1873 (1,46,50,65)

LADD, Constantine - b IN 1847; s William and Isabella (Boyd) Ladd; d 28 Apr 1861 (3,46,50)

LADD, Isabella - b IN 15 Feb 1851; dt Samuel and Charity (Cook) Ladd; mbr Mississinewa MM; d 6 Mar 1876 (1,46,50, 54,65)

LADD, Isabelle (Boyd) - b 26 Apr 1805; dt Samuel and Isabella (Higgins) Boyd; m William Ladd; d 16 Sep 1854 (3,6,25,28,46)

LADD, Samuel - b Wayne Co. 5 Jan 1828; s William and Isabella (Boyd) Ladd; 12 May 1850 m Charity Cook; d 8 Dec 1856 (3,6,10,23,24,28,46)

LADD, William - b Stokes Co., NC 1 Feb 1797; s Joseph and Catherine (Dameron) Ladd; m Isabelle Boyd; d 4 May 1857 (3,6,25,28,46)

LEWIS, Wren 'Renna' (Certain) - dt Henry and Charity E. (McCrum) Certain; 25 Mar 1901 m Charles Lewis; d 28 Jul 1903 at age 25 (14,15,47)

LLOYD, __ - child of M & M Martin Lloyd; d Jun 1897 (12)

LLOYD, Opal - dt Burr and Ida B. Lloyd; d Oct 1898 at age 3y, funeral in Deer Creek Friends MH, prob bur Deer Creek Friends Cem (13,46)

LOWERY, John - d 185_ (3)

LOWERY, Lydial J. - b 1839; d 1882 (3,6,28)

McADOW, Mrs. Elizabeth - d Mar 1897, funeral in Deer Creek Friends MH, prob bur Deer Creek Friends Cem (12)

McCRACKEN, Thomas E. - b 15 Oct 1870; s David and Esther (Allen) McCracken; mbr Deer Creek MM; d 1 Mar 1874 (1,3,64)

McCRUM, James - b Ireland 19 Aug 1812; d Jul 1895 (12)

McINTIRE, Earl - s M & M Joseph McIntire; d 1 Nov 1906 at age 9m (19)

METCALF, Thurlo L. - b 27 Mar 1893; s Thomas Newton and Caroline A. 'Carrie' (Howard) Metcalf; mbr Marion MM; d 23 Jul 1893 (1,11,61)

METCALF, Ethel - b 6 Jul 1878; dt Thomas Newton and Caroline A. 'Carrie' (Howard) Metcalf; mbr Deer Creek MM; d 9 Sep 1879 (1)

MILLER, __ - child of Rome Miller; d Jan 1895 (12)

NEAL, Anna - b 18 Dec 1842; dt Mahlon and Maris (Harris) Neal; mbr Oak Ridge MM; d 11 Sep 1859 (1,46)

OVERLY, Cyrus Clark - s M & M Clark Overly; d Jul 1902, funeral in Deer Creek Friends MH, prob bur Deer Creek Friends Cem (14)

OWEN(s), infant - child of George W. and Rebecca J. (Turner) Owen; d Apr 1892 (10,11)

OWENS, Owens J. - b 2 Mar 1854; d 7 Dec 1893 (3)

OWEN(S), Rebecca J. (Turner) - b IN ca 1854; dt Henry and Margaret (Adkin) Turner; 4 Mar 1872 m George W. Owens; d 18 Dec 1893 (10,11,47,50)

OWINGS, Mrs. Lester - d Jun 1904 (14)

RICHARDSON, Oliver - age 17/18; s Henry T. And Samira J. (Carroll) Richardson; d Jan 1899 (10,13)

SHUGART, Abigail (Osborn) - b NC 8 Dec 1824; dt William and Keziah (Harvey) Osborn; 17 Mar 1846 m George Shugart, Jr.; f mbr Deer Creek Anti-slavery MM; mbr Mississinewa MM; d 29 Sep 1867 (1,3,6,22,24,25,28,46,50,59,65)

SHUGART, Elenora N. - b 25 Aug 1860; dt Cornelius and Harriet T. (Coleman) Shugart; mbr Mississinewa MM; d 1 Jan 1865 (1,46,62,64,65)

SHUGART, George - b NC 30 Aug 1770; s Zachariah and Catharine Shugart; NC, 10 Oct 1793 m Mary Davis; came to Grant Co. 1835; Elder & mbr Deer Creek Anti-slavery MM; d 10 Oct 1851 (1,25,26,46,49,55,59)

SHUGART, Irene - b 1833; prob dt George and Ruth (Marine) Shugart; mbr Mississinewa MM; d 1837, may be first burial in Deer Creek Friends Cem (1,3,6,8,28)

SHUGART, John - b Randolph Co., NC 5 Dec 1795; s George and Mary (Davis) Shugart; 28 Sep 1814 m Sarah Ratliff in Whitewater MH; Elder, Deer Creek Anti-slavery MM; donated 3-acre site of Deer Creek Friends MH, School and Cemetery; d 15 Sep 1853 at age 54 (1,3,6,8,9,25,28,46,49,55,59)

SHUGART, Joseph - b 24 Jan 1849; s John and Rebecca (Guyer) Shugart; mbr Deer Creek MM; d 22 Feb 1870 (1,46)

SHUGART, Lucy Anna - b 12 Sep 1864; dt John and Rebecca (Guyer) Shugart; mbr Deer Creek MM; d 11 Oct 1865 (1,46)

SHUGART, Luzena - b 31 Oct 1854; dt John and Rebecca (Guyer) Shugart; mbr Deer Creek MM; d 18 Sep 1873 (1,46, 64,65)

SHUGART, Mary (Davis) - b Chatham Co., NC 7 Jun 1775; dt John and Mary (Chamness) Davis; 10 Oct 1793 m George Shugart; mbr Deer Creek Anti-slavery MM; d 15 Jul 1848 (1,17,46,55,59,63)

SHUGART, Rachel Jane - b 16 Sep 1850; dt John and Rebecca (Guyer) Shugart; mbr Deer Creek MM; d 22 Mar 1851 (1,46)

SHUGART, Sarah (Ratliff) - b 27 May 1794; dt Cornelius and Elizabeth (Charles) Ratliff; 28 Sep 1814 m John Shugart at

Whitewater Friends MH; f mbr Deer Creek Anti-slavery MM; mbr Deer Creek MM; d 11 Jan 1873 (1,3,11,25,46,55,59,64)

SLODERBECK, Asenith (McCracken) - b IN 11 Sep 1852; dt David and Esther (Allen) McCracken; m Jacob Sloderbeck 12 Nov 1870; mbr Deer Creek MM; d 19 Jan 1873 at age 20y, 1m, 9da (1,3,10,50,64)

SMITH, Margaret J. (Elliott) - b IN; dt Samuel and Mary A. Elliott; 10 Dec 1871 m James W. Smith; d 6 Aug 1872 at age 17y, 1m, 5da (3,10,50)

THOMAS, Joseph - b 28 Dec 1835; s Daniel and Rachel (Way) Thomas; mbr Mississinewa MM, d 1860 (1,3,6,28,46,68,69)

WALTERS, __ - s M & M J.E. Walters; d Oct 1907 (19)

WHITSON, Hiram B. - b 27 Feb 1850; s Amos and Rebecca (Peelle) Whitson; mbr Mississinewa MM; d 6 Nov 1861 (1,62,65)

WHITSON, Willis E. - b IN 27 Jul 1844; s Amos and Rebecca (Peelle) Whitson; f mbr Deer Creek Anti-slavery MM; mbr Mississinewa MM; d Memphis, TN 28 Feb 1863 while serv Co. C, 89th Ind. Inf. (1,2,3,11,23,49,50,65)

WHITSON, Zilpha - b 1 Feb 1833; dt Amos and Rebecca (Peelle) Whitson; mbr Deer Creek Anti-slavery MM; d (1,3,6,8,28)

WOOTON, Lewis - b 2 Dec 1799; m Martha; mbr Deer Creek Anti-slavery MM; d 1850 (1,3,6,8,25,28)

Little Ridge Friends Cemetery is 0.2 miles east of the junction of County Roads 200 West and 1050 South. It is on the south side of C.R. 1050 South and is on the northwest side of the South Chapel of Liberty Friends (formerly Little Ridge Friends meetinghouse). It is located in the W half of the SW quarter of Section 35, Township 23 N, Range 7 E, Liberty Township, Grant County, Indiana. Burials no longer occur in this cemetery.

ALLRED, Albert - b 22 Sep 1872; s George N. and T. Allred; d 27 Jan 1873 (3,4,5,22)

BENNETT, Hester A. - dt Joseph K. and Hester (Sap) Bennett; d 2 Sep 1862 at age 11m, 4da (4,46)

BOYLE, infant - b Aug 1867; dt W. and M.J. Boyle; d Aug 1867 at age 3da (3,4,5)

BREWER, George - b IN 16 Nov 1845; s William and Nancy Brewer; d 14 Dec 1862 while serv as Pvt., Co. C, 89th Ind. Inf. (4,5,22,23,50)

BREWER, Nancy - b 10 Jul 1809; m William Brewer; d 5 Jul 1865 (3,4,5)

BREWER, William - b 28 Mar 1792; m Nancy; d 20 Jan 1878 (3,4,5,22)

BRILES, John - b Randolph Co., NC 13 Jun 1822; m Elizabeth Young; 1865 came to Grant Co.; mbr Fairmount MM; d 5 Dec 1886 (1,3,4,5,24,27)

BUSH, Azel - b NC 4 Aug 1780; m Sarah; mbr Oak Ridge MM; d 30 Aug 1859 (1)

CALDWELL, Train - b IN 7 Apr 1822; m Eliza Wells; d 27 Jul 1881 (3,4,5,25,27,50,54)

COCHRAN, Claudia - b 10 Aug 1884; dt C.H./C.M. and S.C.

Cochran; d 7 Apr 1886 (3,4,5)

DAVIS, Abigail C. - b 8 Feb 1855; dt Kelly W. and Jane Davis; mbr Fairmount MM; d 23 Dec 1873 (1,3,4,5)

DAVIS, Jane - b 7 Dec 1829; m Kelly W. Davis; mbr Fairmount MM; d 10 Dec 1880 (1,4,5,17)

DAVIS, John Ruffin - b NC 15 Dec 1851; s Kelly W. and Jane Davis; 1st m Mary Highfield 16 Feb 1872; 2nd m Mossie Hasting 27 Oct 1889; f mbr Fairmount MM; d 20 Jun 1899 (1,10,13,41)

DAVIS, Kelly W. - b NC 14 Jan 1825; m 1st Jane; m 2nd Lavina Burk 11 Jun 1881; mbr Oak Ridge MM; d 27 Aug 1896 (1,3,4,5,10,12,17,54)

DAVIS, Mary Margaret Abigail - b 30 Sep 1872; dt Murdock L. and Mary Ann Davis; mbr Fairmount MM; d 31 May 1878 (1,3,4,5)

DAVIS, Pasha A. - b 2 Oct 1858; dt Kelly W. and Jane Davis; mbr Fairmount MM; d 25 Feb 1876 (1,3,4,5)

DeGOLYER, __ - twin infants of Albert and Florence DeGolyer; d Aug 1908 (20)

DeGOLYER, __ - child of Albert and Florence DeGolyer; d Sep 1910 at age 5y (20)

DeGOLYER, Josephine - m Albert DeGolyer; d Fairmount 8 May 1915 at age 47y, 3m, 26da; burial cost was paid by Joseph Davis, a Friends Minister (48,58)

FERREE, Sarah - b 10 Jan 1858; dt John and Rebecca (Harvey) Ferree; mbr Oak Ridge MM; d 3 Sep 1859 (1,3,4,5,24,25,60)

FINLEY, Margaret E. - b IN 2 Sep 1853; dt Edward H. and Lydia A. Finley; d 4 May 1868 (3,4,5,50)

GAUNTT, Mary E. - b IN 31 Mar 1852; dt Rhuel J. and Sarah (Bealls) Gauntt; mbr Fairmount MM; d 30 May 1890 (1,11,50)

HARVEY, infant - b 12 Nov 1902; dt Austice M. and Rosa A. (Brewer) Harvey; d 12 Nov 1902 (5,16,47)

HARVEY, Alvin - b 29 Nov 1843; s William J. and Ruth (Hadley) Harvey; mbr Oak Ridge MM; d 15 Jan 1859 (1,3,4,5, 25,59,60)

HARVEY, Cynthia - b 31 Mar 1857; dt Jehu and Rebecca (Reeder) Harvey; mbr Fairmount MM; d 28 Aug 1873 (1,3,4, 5,50)

HARVEY, Eli - b IN 26 Dec 1856; s Mahlon and Zilpha (Hadley) Harvey; m Eunice Trader; mbr Fairmount MM; d 6 May 1891 (1,20,24,41,50,54,56)

HARVEY, Elmina - b 2 Mar 1869; dt Jehu and Rebecca (Reeder) Harvey; mbr Fairmount MM; d 2 Mar 1880 (1,3,4, 5,61)

HARVEY, Hershel Henry - b 30 Jan 1886; s John and Sarah E. (Price) Harvey; mbr Fairmount MM; d 31 Jan 1887 (1)

HARVEY, Hiram H. - may be b 10 Nov 1838; s William J. and Ruth (Hadley) Harvey; mbr Little Ridge MM; d at age 7, perhaps on 13 Aug 1841?; prob bur in Little Ridge Friends Cem (1,25,59)

HARVEY, Jehu/John - b Morgan Co. 11 Jan 1833; s William J. and Ruth (Hadley) Harvey; 20 Sep 1855 m Rebecca Reeder at Little Ridge Friends MH; mbr Fairmount MM; d 22 Apr 1875 (1,3,4,5,25,50,54,59,61,62)

HARVEY, Julia - b 12 Nov 1859; dt Jehu and Rebecca (Reeder) Harvey; mbr Fairmount MM; d 18 Mar 1876 (1,3,4, 5,61)

HARVEY, Rachel Adaline (Wright) - b 20 Apr 1852; dt Jesse and Charity (Reese) Wright; 4 Sep 1873 m Milton Harvey; mbr Fairmount MM; d 22 Jun 1875 (1,3,4,5,10,50)

HARVEY, Ruth (Hadley) - b 25 Aug 1798; dt William and Sarah (Clark) Hadley; m William J. Harvey; mbr Back Creek MM; d 1 Apr 1851 (1,25,43,59,62)

HARVEY, Sarah Emelea/Emlen - b IN 3 Jun 1848; dt Mahlon and Zilpha (Hadley) Harvey; mbr Oak Ridge MM; d 19 Dec 1865 (1,3,4,5,24,50,56)

HARVEY, Therrissa O. - b 20 Aug 1879; dt Eli and Eunice (Trader) Harvey; prob mbr Fairmount MM; d 11 Jan 1884 (1,3,4,5)

HARVEY, William J. - b NC 15 Jun 1791; s Eli and Elizabeth (Carter) Harvey; 11 Jul 1816 m Ruth Hadley at Springfield Friends MH, OH; mbr Fairmount MM; d 10 Mar 1883 (1,3,4,5, 24,25,43,50,54,59,61,66)

HOOVER, David Y. - b NC 8 Dec 1830; m 1st Nettie Rush; 1 Jan 1867 m 2nd Sarah Harvey; m 3rd Rachel Victoria Hoover; CW vet, serv Co. A, 89th Ind. Inf. and/or Corp., Co. F, 34th Ind. Inf. and mbr Fairmount Militia; mbr Fairmount MM; d 24 Apr 1900 (1,2,3,4,5,10,20,22,23,27,41,47,50,54)

HOOVER, Nettie (Rush) - b 9 Jul 1834; m David Y. Hoover as his 1st wife; mbr Fairmount MM; d 6 Sep 1860 (1,3,4,5)

HOOVER, Rachel - b 23 Oct 1856; dt A. and C. Hoover; d 14 Apr 1888 or 1867 (3,4,5)

HOOVER, Sarah (Harvey) - b OH 13 Aug 1823; dt William and Ruth (Hadley) Harvey; 1 Jan 1867 m David Y. Hoover as his 2nd wife; mbr Fairmount MM; d 12 Apr 1888 (1,3,4,5,10, 50,59,61)

LARRANCE, William P. - b 13 Dec 1868; s Thomas H. and
Ann Mariah (Cox) Larrance; mbr Oak Ridge MM; d 30 Jan
1869 (1)

MOON, Isaiah - b OH 2 Feb 1820; s Thomas and Elizabeth
(Hockett) Moon; OH ca Sep 1840 m Mary; 1855 came to Grant
Co.; mbr Oak Ridge MM; d 26 Feb 1904 (1,3,4,5,14,46,50,54,56)

MOON, Martha J. - b OH 3/5 May 1848; dt Isaiah and Mary
Moon; d 25 Jul 1860 (3,4,5,50)

MOON, Mary - b TN 1 Jun 1816; OH m Isaiah Moon ca Sep
1840; d 31 Aug 1886 (3,4,5,30,46,50)

NICOLS, Elish - 1st burial here (26)

PIERCE, Elizabeth Jane - b TN 18 Sep 1835; m George M.
Peirce; mbr Fairmount MM; d 13 Jun 1867 (1,3,4,5,50)

PIERCE, Mary Ann - b IN 29 May 1858; dt George M. and
Elizabeth Jane Pierce; mbr Fairmount MM; d 19 Mar 1861
(1,50)

PHILLIPS, Frances 'Fanny' H. (Caldwell) - b 2 Jul 1854; dt
Train and Eliza (Wells) Caldwell; m John C. Phillips 10 Oct
1872; d 4 Feb 1877 (3,4,5,10,25,50)

PHILLIPS, Malinda W. (Wright) - b TN 3 May 1843; dt Jesse
and Charity (Reese) Wright; 1 Jan 1867 m Josiah Phillips as
his 1st wife; mbr Fairmount MM; d 19 Jan 1876 (1,3,4,5,10,
50,59)

POWELL, Nancy - b 3 Jul 1855; dt John and Sarah (Winslow)
Powell; d 12 Jan 1867 (3,4,5,23)

POWELL, Sarah (Winslow) - b 1 Nov 1831; m John Powell;
may be mbr Back Creek MM; d 23 Dec 1861 (1,3,4,5,17,23)

REEDER, Elizabeth - b 15 Mar 1805; m John J. Reeder; mbr

Back Creek MM; d 29 Jul 1877 (1,3,4,5)

RICHARDSON, Arminda - b 1 Jan 1877; dt Hogan and Mary Richardson; d 24 Aug 1877 (3,4,5,46)

RICHARDSON, Charles S. - b 4 Oct 1868; s Hogan and Mary Richardson; d 14 Sep 1869 (3,4,5,46)

RICHARDSON, Minerva C. - b 2 Sep 1862; dt Hogan and Mary Richardson; d 24 Oct 1864 (4,46)

RUSH, Azel - b 10 Aug 1780; s Benjamin and Dorcas E. (Vickery) Rush; 1806 m Elizabeth Beckerdite; m 2nd Mary 'Polly' White 24 Mar 1819; m 3rd Sarah Young 16 May 1830; mbr Little Ridge MM; d 30 Aug 1859 (1,3,4,5,17,22,23,25,46, 53,60)

RUSH, Sarah 'Sally' (Young) - b Randolph Co., NC 20 Feb 1799; dt Henry Young; 16 May 1830 m Azel Rush; mbr Little Ridge MM; d 21 Feb 1869 (1,3,4,5,46,50)

RUSH, Sarah Alice - b IN 19 Jan 1859; dt Thomas Elwood and Mary (Harvey) Rush; mbr Fairmount MM; d 14 Sep 1873 (1,46,50)

RUSH, Wilson - b 29 Jan 1883; s Miles and Lucy (Wilson) Rush; mbr Fairmount MM; d 7 Dec 1892 (1,22,46)

TRADER, Margaret Adaline - b 22 Dec 1872; dt Robert W. and Phebe Ann (Wright) Trader; mbr Fairmount MM; d 9 Sep 1873 (1,3,4,5,22)

WAGGY, Philip - b VA; m Rachel; serv Co. H, 12th Ind. Inf.; d ca age 40 on 19 May 1862 while home on furlough from army (21,50,56)

WHITE, Simon P. - b 1859; s Jean and Sarah A. White; d 4 Aug 1860 at age 1y, 24da (4,5)

WRIGHT, Alpheas M. - b IN 16 Aug 1854; s Moses and Elizabeth (Hollingsworth) Wright; d 28 Apr 1880 (1,3,4,5,25, 50,66)

WRIGHT, Charles N. - b 25 Dec 1860; s Joel B. and Sarah Jane (Bales) Wright; mbr Oak Ridge MM; d 9 Sep 1861 (1,3,4,5,23, 24,59)

WRIGHT, Charity (Reese) - b 14 Aug 1814; dt John and Phebe Reese; 1831 m Jesse Wright; mbr Oak Ridge MM; d 26 Mar or Sep 1859 (1,3,4,20,23,24,59,60,62)

WRIGHT, Clarence - b 28 Jul 1878; s Joel B. and Adeline Wright; d 1 or 18 Aug 1878 at age 3da (3,4,5,59)

WRIGHT, Cornelius F. - b 28 Jun 1857; s Joel B. and Sarah Jane (Bales) Wright; mbr Oak Ridge MM; d 6 Sep 1858 (1,3,4, 5,23,24,59,60)

WRIGHT, David William - b Grant Co. 27 Feb 1855; s Jesse and Charity (Reese) Wright; mbr Oak Ridge MM; d 24 Jun 1867 (1,3,4,5,24,59)

WRIGHT, Deborah E. - dt Moses T. and Elizabeth (Hollingsworth) Wright; b & d 14 Feb 1864 (66)

WRIGHT, Elizabeth (Hollingsworth) - b OH 3 Jun 1828; dt Henry and Hannah (Zentmeyer) Hollingsworth; 10 May 1847 m Moses T. Wright; mbr Fairmount MM; d 2 May 1892 (1,3,4, 5,25,43,47,50,59,66)

WRIGHT, Hannah (Coggeshall) - b IN 22 Jul 1818; dt Tristam and Elizabeth Coggeshall; m 1st William Jones as his 2nd wife; 21 Feb 1861 m 2nd Jesse Wright as his 2nd wife; mbr Oak Ridge MM; murdered 9 Aug 1873 (1,4,5,20,50)

WRIGHT, Hannah Catherine - b IN 15 May 1851; dt Moses T. and Elizabeth (Hollingsworth) Wright; d 4 Sep 1865 (3,4,5,25, 50,66)

WRIGHT, Harriet E. (Hite) - b IN ca 1841; dt William N. and Sarah Hite; 20 Sep 1873 m Joel B. Wright; d 1874, may be bur here (10,23,50,59)

WRIGHT, Jacob Henry - b IN 15 May 1851; s Moses T. and Elizabeth (Hollingsworth) Wright; mbr Fairmount MM; d 21 May 1891 (1,3,4,5,20,25,41,50,53,59)

WRIGHT, Jemima Ruth - b TN 23 Oct 1838; dt Jesse and Charity (Reese) Wright; was a school tchr; mbr Oak Ridge MM; d 6 Jul 1864 (1,4,5,24,50,59,62)

WRIGHT, Jesse - b Green Co., TN 22 Mar 1810; in 1831 m 1st Charity Reese (dec 1859); m 2nd Hannah (Coggeshall) Jones 21 Feb 1861; m 3rd Mary E.; was a Medical Dr.; mbr Oak Ridge MM; d 8 Aug 1899 (1,3,4,5,13,20,23,24,41,50,54,66)

WRIGHT, Mary E. - b TN 6 Jun 1849; dt Jesse and Charity (Reese) Wright; d 5 Jul or Apr 1866 (3,4,5,24,50)

WRIGHT, Milton R. - b 18 May 1859; s Joel B. and Sarah Jane (Beals) Wright; d 9 Sep 1861, prob bur here (23,50,59)

WRIGHT, Moses Thomas - b TN 11 Dec 1826; s Jacob and Catharine (Reese) Wright; 10 May 1847 m Elizabeth Hollingsworth; d 16 Aug 1865 (1,3,25,43,50,59,66)

WRIGHT, Precious M. - b 10 Mar 1842; dt John and Joanna Wright; mbr Oak Ridge MM; d 18 Nov 1859, may be bur Oak Ridge Friends Cem (1,3,4,5,60)

WRIGHT, Ruth E. - b 30 Apr 1849; dt John and Joanna Wright; mbr Oak Ridge MM; d 16 Nov 1859, may be bur Oak Ridge Friends Cem (1,3,4,5,60)

WRIGHT, Sarah Jane (Beals/Bales) - b Green Co., TN 25 Aug 1836; dt Abner and Serena (Pierce) Bales; 1 Feb 1854 m Joel B. Wright; 1855 moved to Grant Co.; mbr Oak Ridge MM; d 17 Mar 1873 (1,3,4,5,23,50,59)

WRIGHT, William G. - b 16 Aug 1874; s Joel B. and Harriet E. (Hite) Wright; d 22 Dec 1874 (3,4,5,10,23,59)

Oak Ridge Friends Cemetery is on the south side of County Road 800 South just west of C.R. 100 West and is across the road from the North Chapel of Liberty Friends (formerly Oak Ridge Friends meetinghouse). It is located in the NE quarter of the NE quarter of Section 23, Township 23 N, Range 7 E, Liberty Township, Grant County, Indiana. Burials no longer occur in this cemetery.

ALBERT, __ - child of M & M Harry Albert; prob mbr Deer Creek MM; d Mar 1899 (1,13)

ARNETT, Amanda (Rich) - b 26 Feb 1862; dt Elias and Anna (Winslow) Rich; m Lewis Arnett 3 Aug 1884; mbr Oak Ridge MM; d 1897 (1,3,4,46,53)

ARNETT, Eleanor (Jones) - b IN 19 Nov 1834; 18 Aug 1853 m Lindley Arnett; mbr Oak Ridge MM; d 11 Dec 1864 (1,3,4,25, 46,50)

ARNETT, Estelle E. - b 10 Apr 1875; dt Stephen S. and Ruth Ann (Rich) Arnett; mbr Back Creek MM; d 10 Apr 1875 (1,3,4)

ARNETT, Joseph Addison - b 6 Apr 1860; s Lindley and Eleanor (Jones) Arnett; mbr Oak Ridge MM; d 23 Apr 1865 (1,3,4,46,50)

BAKER, Jessie Gladys - b 14 Oct 1920; prob dt Perry J. Baker; d 24 Oct 1924 (48)

BALLARD, Mary Ann (Haisley) - b 25 Mar 1832; dt Jesse and Ruth (Kendall) Haisley; m David F. Ballard; mbr Pipe Creek/ Amboy MM; d 20 Dec 1884 (1,3,4)

BEEMAN, Needam - b NC; 22 Oct 1829 may have 1st m Sally Smith in Henry Co.; 2nd m Abigail; 1846 came to Grant Co.; d 11 Jun 1861 at age 55y, 5m, 16da (3,4,23,27,50,70)

BISHOP, Ezra - b OH 22 May 1817; 1830's came to Grant Co.; m Martha; mbr Oak Ridge MM; d 25 Apr 1873 (1,3,4,23,25,

50,54)

BISHOP, Martha - b IN 12 Oct 1820; m Ezra Bishop; mbr Oak Ridge MM; d 26 Jul 1865 (1,3,4,50,62)

BOND, Anna (Arnett) - b 19 Mar 1843; dt Jesse and Margaret Arnett; m Joshua M. Bond ca 1866; mbr Oak Ridge MM; d (1,8)

BOND, Joshua M. - b 16 Jan 1845; s Mordecai and Rachel (Marshall) Bond; m Anna Arnett ca 1866; mbr Oak Ridge MM; d 30 Jun 1868 (1,8)

BRADBURY, Arrenca O. - dt John T. and Harriet (Fulton) Bradbury; d 8 Jun 1877 at age 9m, 10da (3,4,10)

BRADBURY, John G. - s John T. and Harriet (Fulton) Bradbury; d 20 Feb 1868 at age 7y, 7m, 20da (3,4,10,50)

BRADBURY, Levina May - dt John T. and Harriet (Fulton) Bradbury; d 11 Jan 1876 at age 2m, 14da (3,4,10)

CAREY, Ervin - b 3 Nov 1864; s Jesse Green M. and Jane (Haisley) Carey; mbr Oak Ridge MM; d 20 Sep 1865 (1,46,62)

CAREY, John H. - b OH 10 Jan 1836; s Isaac and Elizabeth (Moon) Carey; mbr Back Creek MM; d 15 Mar 1857 (1,3,4,46, 59,60)

CAREY, John T., Sr. - b PA 22 Jun 1783; s Samuel and Rachel (Doan) Carey; 13 Nov 1805 m Margaret Green at Mt. Pleasant Friends MH, VA; mbr Back Creek MM; d 6 Mar 1854 at age 70y, 8m, 2da (1,3,4,17,25,30,46,53,59,62)

CAREY, Margaret (Green) - b PA 12 Mar 1783; dt John and Ruth (Holloway) Green; 13 Nov 1805 m John T. Carey, Sr.; mbr Oak Ridge MM; d 3 Jun 1866 at age 84y, 20da (1,3,4,17,25, 30,46,53,59)

CAREY, Sarah Ann (Haisley) - b 21 Sep 1841; dt Eri and
Emma (Williams) Haisley; 24 Mar 1858 m William M. Carey
at Oak Ridge MH; mbr Back Creek MM; d 6 Dec 1865 (1,3,4,46,
50,62)

CARTER, Lydia Ann (Andrew) - b 13 May 1848; dt William
and Ruth (Garner) Andrew; OH ca Apr 1866 m Samuel
Carter; mbr Oak Ridge MM; d 13 Jul 1888 at age 40y, 2m (1,3,4,
11,30)

CHEW, Martha - d 10 Aug 1870 at age 65y, 7m, 8da (3,4)

CHOPSON, Elizabeth - b 1759; m William Chopson; d 18 Jan
1870 at age 110y, 9m (4,25,25)

COMER, Lavina (Peacock) - b IN 9 Feb 1842; dt William and
Phoebe (Haisley) Peacock; 23 Mar 1864 m Aaron Comer in
Oak Ridge Friends MH; mbr Fairmount MM; d 16 May 1874
(1,3,4,21,25,46,50,59)

CONGER/CONGAR, Wesley M. - b VA; d 12 Apr or 13 Nov
1861 at age 26y, 2m, 4da (3,4,50)

COX, Arlendo J. - s W. and S.M. Cox; d 22 Nov or 16 Jan 1865
at age 1y, 3m, 11da (3,4)

COX, Elizabeth - b NC 13 Aug 1831; dt William and Miriam
(Winslow) Cox; mbr Back Creek MM; d 22 Apr 1861 (1,3,4,
50,60)

COX, Emily - b 10 Dec 1837; dt William and Miriam (Winslow) Cox; mbr Back Creek MM; d of typhoid fever 11/14 Oct
1855 (1,3,4,62)

COX, Miriam (Winslow) - b 26 Feb 1807; dt Henry and Elizabeth (Needdom) Winslow; NC m William Cox 15 Jan 1829;
mbr Back Creek MM; d 9 Nov 1855 (1,3,4,17)

COX, Samuel - b NC 12 Jun 1812; s John William and Lydia

(Littler) Cox; NC m Asenath J. Hobson ca 1863; mbr Fairmount MM; d 8 May 1874 (1,4,17)

COX, William - b NC 22 Apr 1803; s John William and Lydia (Littler); NC m Miriam Winslow 15 Jan 1829; mbr Back Creek MM; d 8 Jun 1867 (1,3,4,17)

DAVIDSON, Nathan - b MD 28 Mar 1840; s George and Lydia Davidson; mbr Oak Ridge MM; d 13 Nov 1864 (1,3,4,50,62)

DAVIS, __ - d May 1851 (4)

DAVIS, Charlotte (Baldwin) - b NC 11 May 1823; dt John and Charlotte (Payne) Baldwin; 15 Dec 1841 m George Davis; mbr Oak Ridge MM; d 6 Dec 1882 (1,3,4,24,50,55,59); may be bur in Mississinewa Friends Cem (29)

DAVIS, John F. - b IN 12 Feb 1850; s George and Charlotte (Baldwin) Davis; mbr Oak Ridge MM; d 3 Feb 1864 (1,24,50)

DAVIS, Melissa - b IN 12 Feb 1850; dt George and Charlotte (Baldwin) Davis; mbr Oak Ridge MM; d 21 Aug 1861 (1,24, 50,59); may be bur in Mississinewa Friends Cem (29)

DOHERTY, Orval - b 3 Jul 1875; s John M. and Mary R. (Davis) Doherty; mbr Oak Ridge MM; d 3 Jul 1875 (1,24,59)

EDINGTON, Silvania F. - dt Samuel and Elizabeth Edington; d 5 Dec 1866 at age 6y, 2m, 29da (3,4)

FELTON, Elizabeth (Brightwell) - b PA ca 1808; Butler Co., OH m John Felton 11 Jan 1821; d 26 Feb 1881 at age 70y, 3m, 15da (3,4,21,46,50,53)

FELTON, Harrison - b IN 2 Jun 1835; s John and Elizabeth (Brightwell) Felton; d 2 Aug 1867 (3,4,46,50)

FELTON, John - b KY 15 Feb 1796; s William and Margaret (Mansfield) Felton; 1st m Elizabeth Brightwell 11 Jan 1821;

came to Grant Co. 1839; 2nd m Elizabeth Murray; d 15 Apr 1878 at age 81y, 2m (3,4,21,23,46,50,53,54)

GAUNTT, Kerenhappoch - b TN; mbr Back Creek MM; d 5 Jun 1849 at age 32y, 4m, 28da (1,3,4)

GAUNTT, Precious (Pugh) - b SC 7 Nov 1790; dt Azariah and Lydia Pugh; m Samuel K. Gauntt ca 1818; d 24 Jan 1852 at age 61y, 2m, 7da (3,4,11,23,41)

GAUNTT, Precious R. - dt Reuel Julian and Sarah (Bealls) Gauntt; d 6 Dec 1856 at age 3m, 5da (3,4,11,23)

GAUNTT, Reuel Julian - b Green Co., TN 17 Jul 1824; s Samuel K. and Precious (Pugh) Gauntt; Grant Co. 7 Nov 1847 m Sarah Bealls; 1849 came to Grant Co.; mbr Fairmount MM; d 27 Jul 1889 (1,11,20,23,24,41,50)

GAUNTT, Samuel Kelly - s Samuel and Abigail (Kelly) Gaunt; m Precious Pugh ca 1818; d 12 Jun 1856 at age 69y, 11m, 7da (3,4,11,17,23,24,41)

HAISLEY, infant - b 1 Jan 1861; child of Eri and Emma (Williams) Haisley; d 21 Jan 1861 (46)

HAISLEY, Albert - b 19 Nov 1870; s David and Elmira (Rich) Haisley; mbr Oak Ridge MM; d 19 Nov 1870 (1,3,4,46)

HAISLEY, Allen - b 26 Feb 1828; s Jesse and Ruth (Kendall) Haisley; 19 Sep 1849 m Mary Overman; mbr Oak Ridge MM; d 8 Aug 1857 (1,3,4,46,60)

HAISLEY, Alva - b 17 Feb 1857; s Eli and Sally Ann (Mendenhall) Haisley; mbr Back Creek MM; d 15 Mar 1857 (1,3,4,46)

HAISLEY, Alvin - b 17 Feb 1857; s Eli and Sally Ann (Mendenhall) Haisley; mbr Back Creek MM; d 14 May 1857 (1,3,4,46)

HAISLEY, Amanda Jane - b 15 Aug 1867; dt David and Elmira (Rich) Haisley; mbr Oak Ridge MM; d 15 Jan 1876 (1,3, 4,46)

HAISLEY, Calvin - b 14 Aug 1846; s John and Ann (Hawkins) Haisley; mbr Oak Ridge MM; d 5 Oct 1865 (1,24,46,50,59,62)

HAISLEY, Elvina - b 17 Feb 1850; dt Eri and Emma (Williams) Haisley; mbr Oak Ridge MM; d 6 Apr 1853 (1,3,4,46)

HAISLEY, Eri - b IN 24 Dec 1820; s Jesse and Ruth (Kendall) Haisley; 20 Aug 1840 m Emma Williams; mbr Oak Ridge MM; d 6 Jun 1870 (1,3,4,46,54)

HAISLEY, Hannah (Hawkins) - b IN 14 Jun 1824; dt Henry and Phebe Hawkins; at Dover Friends MH 1 Dec 1841 m Cyrus Haisley as his 1st wife; mbr Oak Ridge MM; d 25 Aug 1865 (1,3,4,8,46,50,62)

HAISLEY, Hannah - b 18 Aug 1865; dt Cyrus and Hannah (Hawkins) Haisley; mbr Oak Ridge MM; d 10 Sep 1865 (1,3,4,46)

HAISLEY, Ira - b NC 19 Nov 1815; s Jesse and Ruth (Kendall) Haisley; 23 Mar 1837 m Rebecca Overman; 1838 came to Grant Co.; mbr Oak Ridge MM; d 13 Nov 1888 (1,3,4,11,23,27, 46,50,53,54,59)

HAISLEY, John - b NC 7 Nov 1817; s Jesse and Ruth (Kendall) Haisley; 13 May 1838 m Anna Hawkins at Dover Friends MH; mbr Mississinewa MM; d 6 Nov 1879, may be bur in Mississinewa Friends Cem (1,8,12,24,25,27,46,50,59)

HAISLEY, Manerva - b 6 Dec 1864; dt Eri and Emma (Williams) Haisley; mbr Oak Ridge MM; d 9 Mar 1865 (1,46)

HAISLEY, Margaretta - b 13 Aug 1861; dt Eli and Sally Ann (Mendenhall) Haisley; mbr Oak Ridge MM; d 29 Aug 1861 (1,3,4,46,59,60)

HAISLEY, Maryetta - b 13 Aug 1861; dt Eli and Sally Ann (Mendenhall) Haisley; mbr Oak Ridge MM; d 29 Aug 1861 (1,3,4,46,59,60)

HAISLEY, Milton W. - b 23 Jan 1844; s Eri and Emma (Williams) Haisley; mbr Oak Ridge MM; d 2 Aug 1860 (1,3,4, 46,50,59,60,62)

HAISLEY, Ralph - b 6 Jun 1882; s Harvey and Olive (Moon) Haisley; mbr Oak Ridge MM; d 21 Jun 1883 (1,46)

HAISLEY, Rebecca (Overman) - b Preble Co., OH 11 May 1819; dt Jesse and Keziah (Stubbs) Overman; 23 Mar 1837 m Ira Haisley; mbr Oak Ridge MM; d 18 Feb 1897 (1,3,4,12,23,27,46, 50,53,59)

HAISLEY, Ruth (Kendall) - b NC 27 Feb 1792; dt John and Ann Kendall; m Jesse Haisley 6 Oct 1813; mbr & Elder, Oak Ridge MM; d 11 Nov 1864 (1,3,4,17,23,36,50,62)

HAISLEY, Sally Ann (Mendenhall) - b 20 Feb 1825; dt Jonathan and Ann (Phillips) Mendenhall; m Eli Haisley 15 Jan 1851 at Fairfield Friends MH; mbr Oak Ridge MM; d 13 Aug 1861 (1,3,4,33,46,59,60,62)

HAISLEY, Sanford - b 28 Apr 1859; s Eri and Emma (Williams) Haisley; mbr Oak Ridge MM; d 2 Sep 1859 (1,3,4,46,60)

HAISLEY, Wilson - b 3 Sep 1858; s Eli and Sally Ann (Mendenhall) Haisley; mbr Oak Ridge MM; d 20 Aug 1860 (1,3,4, 46,60)

HARRIS, Branson - mbr Oak Ridge MM; d ca 17 Jun 1928 at age 72 (1,58)

HARROLD, Rebecca - m William Harrold; d 26 May 1852 at age 36 (3,4)

HARVEY, Ruth (Hadley) - b 25 Aug 1798; dt William and

Sarah (Clark) Hadley; 1816 m William J. Harvey at Springfield Friends MH, OH; mbr Back Creek MM; d 1 Apr 1851, prob bur in Little Ridge Friends Cem (1,3,4,23,59,62,66)

HOCKETT, Hannah Ann - b 3 Jul 1867; dt Joseph and Phoebe Ann (Haisley) Hockett; mbr Oak Ridge MM; d 28 Sep 1886 (1,3,4)

HOCKETT, Josiah - b OH 21 Sep 1815; s Joseph and Ruth Hockett; m Mary Milner ca Mar 1835; mbr Oak Ridge MM; d 1894 (1,4,30,46,50)

HOCKETT, Mary (Milner) - b OH 20 Apr 1816; m Josiah Hockett ca Mar 1835; mbr Oak Ridge MM; d 1892 (1,4,30,50)

HOWELL, infant - child of Elsie Howell; d ca 18 Jan 1891 (20,41)

HOWELL, Jeremiah - b Clinton Co., OH 5 Nov 1820; s Benjamin and Elizabeth (Kimbrough) Howell; 1st m Sarah Jenette Jessup 11 Nov 1841; came to Grant Co. 1843; 2nd m Thirza Arnett 19 Aug 1863 at Oak Ridge Friends MH; f mbr Oak Ridge MM; d 14 Nov 1889, funeral in Oak Ridge Friends MH, prob bur Oak Ridge Friends Cem (1,11,21,23,25,41,50,53, 54,59,73)

HOWELL, Jeremiah J. - b 2 Jul 1872; s Charles and Sarah E. (Carey) Howell; mbr Oak Ridge MM; d 26 Apr 1874 (1)

HOWELL, Sarah Jenette (Jessup) - b CT 8 Aug 1823; Clinton Co., OH m Jeremiah Howell 11 Nov 1841; came to Grant Co. in 1843; mbr Oak Ridge MM; d 18 Aug 1862 (1,21,23,50,59, 60,62)

HULL, Mary E. - dt J. and Mary Hull; d 10 Nov 1858 at age 7y, 1m, 4da (3,4)

JAY, Alton - b 27 Dec 1878; s Riley and Anzonetta (Haisley) Jay; mbr Oak Ridge MM; d 15 Apr 1879 (1,3,4,46)

JAY, Clarabell - b 27 Nov 1873; dt Riley and Anzonetta (Haisley) Jay; mbr Oak Ridge MM; d 8 Dec 1882 (1,3,4,46,61)

JAY, Hattie - b 2 Sep 1876; dt Riley and Anzonetta (Haisley) Jay; mbr Oak Ridge MM; d 14 Dec 1882 (1,3,4,46,61)

JOHNSON, __ - s M & M Emanuel Johnson; d Jun 1895 at age 14y (12)

JOHNSON, Garretson - b PA 17 Sep 1820; s Samuel Johnson; m Lydia; d 13 Jun 1861 (3,4,50,53)

JOHNSON, Joseph - s Garretson and Lydia Johnson; d 6 Apr 1874 at age 17y, 3m, 21da (4)

JOHNSON, Lydia - b PA; m Garretson Johnson; d 11 Jul 1871 at age 47y, 3m, 1da (3,4,50,53,54)

JOHNSON, Samuel - b PA 1784; d 18 __ 1863 at age 79y, _m, 11da (4,50,53)

JONES, infant - b 22 Mar 1867; s Lewis and Mary E. (Kirk) Jones; d 22 Mar 1867 (4,10)

JONES, infant - b 12 Mar 1875; s Calvin W. and Caroline (Haisley) Jones; mbr Oak Ridge MM; d 16 Mar 1875 (1,4,46)

JONES, Caroline (Haisley) - b IN 22 Jul 1851; dt Ira and Rebecca (Overman) Haisley; 18 Apr 1870 m Calvin W. Jones as his 1st wife; mbr Oak Ridge MM; d 26 Mar 1875 (1,3,4,46,50)

JONES, Delfina A. - b 21 Sep 1864; dt Thomas and Mariah (Miller) Jones; d 22 Sep 1864 (3,4,10,23)

JONES, George M. - b Apr 1867; s Thomas and Mariah (Miller) Jones; 13 Mar 1892 m Elizabeth Jane Elliott; f mbr Oak Ridge MM (1,4,10,21,23,46,53)

JONES, John A. - b Liberty Twp. 29 Mar 1863/1866; s Thomas

and Mariah (Miller) Jones; m Frances K. Faust; f mbr Oak Ridge MM (1,4,10,23,25,46,53,56)

JONES, Lewis - b 6 Mar 1845; s Jonathan and Dorcas (Rush) Jones <u>or</u> s Lewis and Mary (Dunbar) Jones; mbr Oak Ridge MM until 1864 disowned because of serv in Co. F, 34th Ind. Inf.; 17 Dec 1865 m Mary Elma Kirk; d 23 Apr 1869 (1,2,3,4,21, 24,25,46)

JONES, Mariah (Miller) - b Licking Co., OH 23 Jan 1834; dt William and Margaret (Chopson) Miller; m Thomas Jones 11 Sep 1856; f mbr Oak Ridge MM; d 21 Apr 1921 at age 87y, 2m, 28da (1,3,4,23,25,46,50,53)

JONES, Mary - dt A.W. and G.A. Jones; d 25 Aug 1861 at age 3y, 11m, 20da (4)

JONES, Seraphina A. - b 15 Jun 1857; dt Thomas and Mariah (Miller) Jones; d 30 Jan 1864 at age 6y, 7m, 15da (3,4,10,23,46)

JONES, Thomas - b Grant Co. 10 Aug 1833; s Jonathan and Dorcas (Rush) Jones <u>or</u> s Lewis and Mary Jones; m Mariah Miller 11 Sep 1856; serv 42nd Ind. Inf. and/or Co. A, 71st Regmt. (6th Cav.) during CW; mbr Oak Ridge MM; d 29 Dec 1875 at age 42y, 5m, 19da (2,3,4,10,21,23,25,46,50,53,54)

KIRK, Alton - s Samuel M. and Mary (Murray) Kirk; prob mbr Oak Ridge MM; d 11 Sep 1879 at age 5m, 19da (1,3,4, 10,25)

LARRENCE, William F. - b 13 Dec 1868; s Thomas H. and Ann Mariah (Cox) Larrence; mbr Oak Ridge MM; d 30 Jan 1869, may be bur Little Ridge Friends Cem (1,3,4)

LEACH, Edmon - b 6 Oct 1869; s John B. and Mary Jane Leach; mbr Oak Ridge MM; d 7 Jan 1870 (1)

LEWIS, Clarence O. - s Thomas W. and Angeline (Bishop) Lewis; d 11 Aug 1873/1875 at age 2m, 8da (1,3,4,10)

LONG, Charles Elwood - b 3 May 1879; s James and Jane (Rich) Long; mbr Oak Ridge MM; d Dec 1881 (1)

LONG, Elizabeth - b 3 Nov 1876; dt James and Jane (Rich) Long; mbr Fairmount MM; d Dec 1904 (1,14,20,56)

McCAN, Anne - m W.F. McCan; d 22 Aug 1887 at age 66y, 3m, 15da (3,4)

McPHERSON, Eleanor (Jones) - b IN 17 Oct 1836; dt Lewis and Mary Jones; 25 Oct 1854 m Daniel McPherson at Oak Ridge Friends MH; mbr Oak Ridge MM; d 18 Jul 1863 (1,3, 4,50)

McPHERSON, Joseph - b VA 14 Jul 1808; m Ruth Carey; mbr Oak Ridge MM; d 27 Aug 1862 (1,3,4,50,59,62)

McPHERSON, Ruth Ann - b 19 Sep 1859; dt Daniel and Eleanor (Jones) McPherson; mbr Oak Ridge MM; d 14 Nov 1859 (1,3,4,60)

McPHERSON, Winslow D. - b 18 Nov 1860; s Daniel and Eleanor (Jones) McPherson; mbr Oak Ridge MM; d 1 Jan 1861 (1,3,4)

MART, Mary (Clark) - b OH; 7 Jun 1861 m Joseph J. Mart; d 2 Jun 186_ at age 23y (3,4,10,25,50)

MART, Samuel A. - s John W. and Sarah J. (Achor) Mart; d 13/23 Jan 1870 at age 1y, 6da (1,3,4,10,11)

MENDENHALL, Eunice Jane - b 3 Apr 1865; dt Jesse H. and Hannah M. (Carey) Mendenhall, mbr Oak Ridge MM (1,4)

MENDENHALL, John - b NC 2 Jan 1813; s Jonathan and Ann Mendenhall; m Mary Ann Cook; mbr Oak Ridge MM; d 12 Oct 1886 (1,50)

MILLER, Isaiah - b PA 30 Aug 1830; s William M. and

Margaret (Chopsin) Miller; m Susannah H.; mbr Oak Ridge MM; d 27 Jul 1892 (1,3,4,11,20,41,50)

MILLER, Margaret (Chopsin) - b VA; m William M. Miller; mbr W.M. Ch.; d 27 Nov 1870 at age 71y, 1m, 27da (1,3,4,23,25, 50,54)

MILLER, William M. - b PA; m Margaret Chopsin; 1843 came to IN; mbr W.M. Ch.; d 4 Jun 1865 at age 69y, 5m, 4da (1,3,4, 23,25)

MILLIKAN, Charles L. - s Isaac S. and Melinda H. (Scott) Millikan; mbr Oak Ridge MM; d 23 Feb 1885 at age 3m, 10da (1,3,4)

MILNER, Josiah - b 1815; m Mary; d 1894 (3)

MILNER, Mary - b 1816; m Josiah Milner; d 1892 (3,4)

MOON, infant - b 31 Jul 1869; child of Nathan B. and Mary Ann (Haisley) Moon; mbr Oak Ridge MM; d 31 Jul 1869 (1,3,4,46,67)

MOON, Isaac - d Feb 1904 at age 84 (14)

MOON, Jacob - b OH 31 May 1823; s Thomas and Elizabeth (Hockett) Moon; m Hannah ca Mar 1848; f mbr Oak Ridge MM; d after 1860 (1,30,46,50)

MOON, Leah Schooley (Harrold) - b NC 27 Oct 1827; dt Andrew and Mary L. (Harrold) Harrold; m Nathan Brown Moon 1 Apr 1847; mbr Oak Ridge MM; d 7 Oct 1865 (1,3,4,8, 30,46,50,62,67)

MOON, Nathan Brown - b OH 8 Jul 1825; s Thomas and Elizabeth (Hockett) Moon; 1st m Leah S. Harrold 1 Apr 1847; 19 Dec 1866 m Mary Ann Haisley at Oak Ridge MH; mbr Oak Ridge MM; d 27 Sep 1869 (1,3,4,46,50,67)

MURRAY, infant - b 3 Dec 1879; dt Andrew and Penina (Beeman) Murray; d 3 Dec 1879 (3,4,10)

MURRAY, Penina (Beeman) - b IN 1 Sep 1835; 1 Jul 1853 m Andrew Murray; d 8 Aug 1886 at age 45y, 11m, 7da (3,4,10,21, 25,50)

MURRAY, Willie - s Andrew and Penina (Beeman) Murray; d 25 Jan 1866 at age 1m (3,4,10)

MURRAY, Willis - s Andrew and Penina (Beeman) Murray; d 27 Jan 1866 at age 1m, 1da (3,4,10)

NEAL, Anna (Ballinger) - b TN 8 Feb 1777; dt James and Lydia (Taylor) Ballinger; m James Neal; mbr Oak Ridge MM; d 26 Apr 1856 (1,3,4,11,18,23,46,71)

NEAL, Charles A. - b 3 Jan 1863; s Thomas H. and Elmina (Arnett) Neal; mbr Oak Ridge MM; d 1 May 1874 (1,3,4,46,61)

NEAL, Clement A. - b 27 Oct 1872; s Thomas H. and Elmina (Arnett) Neal; mbr Oak Ridge MM; d 14 May 1873 (1,4,46)

NEAL, James E. - b 2 Apr 1864; s Thomas H. and Elmina (Arnett) Neal; mbr Oak Ridge MM; d 2 Sep 1865 (1,3,4,46)

NEAL, Mahlon - b TN 13 Nov 1785; s William and Rachel Neal; 9 Apr 1823 m Rachel Duncan in Union Friends MH, OH; 1837 came to Grant Co.; mbr Back Creek MM; d 22 Jul 1851 (1,3,4,11,18,23,59,62,71)

NEAL, Rachel (Duncan) - b SC 15 Apr 1792; dt Samuel and Mary (Embree) Duncan; 9 Apr 1823 m Mahlon Neal in Union Friends MH, OH; mbr Back Creek MM; d 25 Jul 1888 (1,3,4,11,17,18,23,46,59,71)

NEAL, Thomas H. - b IN 30 Jan 1841; s Mahlon and Maris (Harris) Neal; 9 Feb 1862 m Elmina Arnett; mbr Oak Ridge MM; Friends Minister; d 22 Jan 1874 (1,3,4,46,50,54,61)

PARTIDA, Jose - b Mexico 1902; d 1930 (4)

PEACOCK, Amos/Amoz - b 28 Dec 1849; s Joseph and
Caroline (Jones) Peacock; mbr Oak Ridge MM; d 4 Sep 1850
(1,3,4,46)

PEACOCK, Asa - b SC Jun 1790; NC 1st m Dinah Rich; 2nd m
Dorcas (Hale) Jones 13 Oct 1853; mbr Oak Ridge MM; d 23 Feb
1872 (1,21,46,50,54,59)

PEACOCK, John - b 24 Sep 1817; s Asa and Dinah (Rich) Peacock; m Abigail Baldwin 25 Apr 1839 at Back Creek Friends
MH; mbr Back Creek MM; d 1 Sep 1851 (1,46,53,62)

PEACOCK, Joseph H. - b Grant Co. 9 Feb 1844; s William and
Phoebe (Haisley) Peacock; m Elizabeth S. Radley 24 Mar 1869
at Back Creek Friends MH; mbr & Overseer, Fairmount MM;
d 14 May 1874 (1,3,4,21,24,46,50,54,59,61)

PEACOCK, Levi J. - b IN 6 Oct 1857; s William and Phoebe
(Haisley) Peacock; mbr Oak Ridge MM; d 7 Aug 1860 (1,3,4,21,
25,46,50,60,62)

PEACOCK, Lucy - b 13 Mar 1850; dt John and Abigail
(Baldwin) Peacock; mbr Back Creek MM; d 5 Aug 1851
(1,46,53)

PEACOCK, Phoebe (Haisley) - b NC 10 Sep 1812; dt Joseph
and Sarah Haisley; m William Peacock at Concord Friends
MH 23 Aug 1833; mbr Oak Ridge MM; d 23 Mar 1867 (1,8,21,
25,46,50,59)

PEACOCK, Sarah M. - b 21 Sep 1849; dt William and Phoebe
(Haisley) Peacock; mbr Oak Ridge MM; d 17 Apr 1851 (1,3,4,
21,25,46)

PEACOCK, William - b NC 11 Apr 1812; s Asa and Dinah
(Rich) Peacock; m Phoebe Haisley 23 Aug 1833 at Concord
Friends MH; mbr Oak Ridge MM; d 31 Apr 1867 (1,3,4,8,21,24,

25,46,50,59)

PEREZ, Mary Louise - b TX 24 Apr 1937; dt Victor and
Clenimca Vera Perez; d 20 Aug 1938 (48)

POWELL, Hannah (Miller) - 2 Nov 1854 m Thomas H.
Powell; d 5 Jun 1861 at age 31y, 9m, 23da (3,4,10,46)

POWELL, Mary - b IN 1844; dt Harrison and Nancy (Hale)
Powell; d 4 Dec 1861 at age 17y, 11m, 15da (3,4,10,46,50)

PUGH, Lydia - b TN 21 Oct 1764; m Azariah Pugh; mbr Oak
Ridge MM; d 12 Sep 1858 (1,3,4,23,60,62)

REEDER, Emaline - b IN 4 Jul 1841; dt Spencer and Guelma
Julia (Cox) Reeder; mbr Oak Ridge MM; d 23 Dec 1860 (1,3,4,
50,60,62)

REEDER, Guelma Julia (Cox) - b NC 18 Nov 1809; dt John
William and Lydia (Littler) Cox; NC m Spencer Reeder ca
1836; moved NC to IN 1837; mbr Oak Ridge MM; d 5 Feb 1880
(1,11,17,25,50,61)

REEDER, Martha E. - b IN 3 Mar 1857; dt Spencer and Julia
(Cox) Reeder; mbr Oak Ridge MM; d 3 Nov 1875 (1,3,4,50)

REEDER, Spencer - b NC 30 Jun 1814; NC m Guelma Julia
Cox ca 1836; moved NC to IN 1837; mbr Oak Ridge MM; d 12
Mar 1880 (1,11,17,24,25,50,61)

RICH, infant - s Alson W. and R. Rich; d 23 Feb 1894 (3,4)

RICH, infant - s Alson W. and R. Rich; d 16 Aug 1899 (3,4)

RICH, Anna (Winslow) - b NC 12 May 1823; dt Eleazar and
Elizabeth (Stanton) Winslow; m Elias Rich; mbr Oak Ridge
MM; d 11 Dec 1894 (1,3,4,46,50,53)

RICH, Elizabeth - b IN 6 May 1850; dt Elias and Anna (Winslow) Rich; mbr Oak Ridge MM; d 11 Apr 1871 (1,3,4,46,50,54)

RITTENHOUSE, Emery - (21)

RITTENHOUSE, George W. - m Elizabeth Faris; d 4/14 Mar 1884 at age 56y, 1m, 6da (1,3,4)

SAMMS, Albert T. - b 17 Feb 1878; s Aaron and Elmina (Arnett) Samms; mbr Oak Ridge MM; d 17 Aug 1878 (1,3,4)

SAMMS, Elmina (Arnett) - b 17 Apr 1840; dt Jesse and Margaret (Williams) Arnett; 2 Sep 1876 m Aaron Samms; mbr Oak Ridge MM; d 19 Nov 1892 (1,3,4,46,47,50)

SCOTT, Ancel S. - b 20 May 1869; s William and Susannah M. (Carey) Scott; mbr Oak Ridge MM; d 27 Sep 1870 (1,46)

SCOTT, Calvin - b IN 8 Oct 1841; s James and Annis (Arnett) Scott; m Elizabeth Ann Davis 30 Mar 1867; mbr Oak Ridge MM; d 13 Sep 1874 (1,21,46,50,54,59)

SCOTT, Elam - b 29 Jan 1840; s James and Annis (Arnett) Scott; mbr Back Creek MM; d 2 Aug 1849 (1,21,46)

SCOTT, Elizabeth Ann (Davis) - b IN 15 Sep 1842; dt George and Charlotte (Baldwin) Davis; m Calvin Scott 30 Mar 1867; mbr Oak Ridge MM; d 24 Jan 1875 (1,24,46,50,59)

SCOTT, Evy - b 10 Jul 1868; dt Stephen, Jr. and Martha (Cox) Scott; mbr Oak Ridge MM; d 10 Jul 1868 (1,46)

SCOTT, Gladys - dt John L. and Rachel Ann Scott; d 14 Oct 1895 at age 5m, 21da (3,4,12,46)

SCOTT, Golden Marion - dt John L. and Rachel Ann Scott; d 22 Jul 1891 at age 10m, 22da (3,4,11,46)

SCOTT, Iona - b 6 Sep 1896; dt George D. and Ida B. (Jones) Scott; mbr Oak Ridge MM; d 19 Sep 1896 (1,46)

SCOTT, Mahala (Arnett) - b 22 Jan 1823; dt Jesse and Margaret (Williams) Arnett; 23 Sep 1841 m Stephen Scott at Concord Friends MH; 1849 came to Liberty Twp.; mbr Back Creek MM; d 25 Oct 1856 (1,8,20,22,23,41,46)

SCOTT, Martha (Cox) - b IN 17 Feb 1846; dt William and Miriam (Winslow) Cox; 7 Sep 1867 m Stephen Scott, Jr.; mbr Oak Ridge MM; d Wabash Co. 9 Dec 1883 (1,3,4,10,50,61)

SCOTT, Mary Etta - b 4 Sep 1870; dt Elwood and Susanna (Haisley) Scott; mbr Oak Ridge MM; d 14 Dec 1870 (1,46)

SCOTT, Rachel (Horton) - b 4 Nov 1778; dt James and Margaret (Beals) Horton; 10 May 1804 m John Scott; prob mbr Dover MM; d 29 Apr 1857 (3,4,8,46)

SCOTT, Silvester - b 9 Sep 1865; s Eli and Eleanor (Reeder) Scott; mbr Oak Ridge MM; d 11 Nov 1867 (1,46)

SCOTT, Stephen - b Wayne Co. 7 Jul 1821; s John and Rachel (Horton) Scott; 23 Sep 1841 m Mahala Arnett at Concord Friends MH; 1849 came to Liberty Twp.; mbr Oak Ridge MM; d 1 Nov 1889 (1,8,11,20,23,41,46,54)

THOMPSON, Elizabeth - d 18 Jan 1870 at age 11y, 9m (3,4)

WALL, __ - dt Britton and Martha Wall; mbr Back Creek MM; 1st burial in Oak Ridge Friends Cem (1,25)

WALL, Thomas Edmund - b 1864; mbr Oak Ridge MM; d 3 Oct 1919 (1,3,4)

WALL, Mary Jane - b 23 Mar 1857; dt Alson R. and Elizabeth Wall; mbr Oak Ridge MM; d 20 Apr 1857 (1)

WALL, Pharaba - b 3 Jul 1861; dt Alson R. and Elizabeth Wall; mbr Oak Ridge MM; d 30 Jul 1862 (1)

WILLSON, Esther - m __; d 20 May 1891 at age 45 (11,47)

WINSLOW, Sarah (Neal) - b Miami Co., OH 26 Mar 1811; dt James and Anna (Ballinger) Neal; father d OH; 1837 Sarah came to Grant Co. with her mother; 21 Oct 1841 m William Winslow; mbr Back Creek MM; d 28 Aug 1888 (1,3,4,11,18,46)

WRIGHT, infant - b Feb 1871; dt W.R. and H.P. Wright; d Feb 1871 (4)

WRIGHT, Precious M. - b 10 Mar 1842; dt John and Joanna W. Wright; mbr Oak Ridge MM; d 18 Nov 1859 (1)

WRIGHT, Ruth E. - b 19 Apr 1849; dt John and Joanna W. Wright; mbr Oak Ridge MM; d 6 Nov 1859 (1)

YALE, Lovalie - dt George S. and Sophia (Rich) Yale; mbr Oak Ridge MM; d 1 Apr 1887 (1,3,4,21)

1. Heiss, W. 1970. Abstracts of the records of the Society of Friends in Indiana, Part Three. Indiana Historical Society, Indianapolis. 553 pp.
2. Nelson, J.S. 1991. Indiana Quakers confront the Civil War. Indiana Historical Society, Indianapolis. 303 pp.
3. Kendall, Mrs. J.W. No date. Cemetery records of Grant County, Indiana, Vol. 1. Daughters of the American Revolution. not paginated.
4. Watson, S.D. 1996. Cemeteries of Liberty Township, Grant County, Indiana. Loose-leaf. 52 pp.
5. Little Ridge Cemetery. Undated one page loose-leaf in Marion Public Library, Marion, IN.
6. Deer Creek Cemetery. Undated two pages loose-leaf in Marion Public Library, Marion, IN.
7. Friends Cemetery, Marion, Indiana also labeled 'Old Burying Ground.' Undated large plat on one sheet in Marion Public Library, Marion, IN.
8. Heiss, W. 1965. Abstracts of the records of the Society of Friends in Indiana, Part Two. Indiana Historical Society, Indianapolis. 431 pp.
9. Dorrel, R., and T.D. Hamm. 1996. Abstracts of the records of the Society of Friends in Indiana, Vol. 1. Indiana Historical Society, Indianapolis. 318 pp.
10. Grant County, Indiana marriage records, Vol. I, Sept 1831 - Apr 1882. Compiled 1985 by members of Grant County Genealogy Club. Selby Publishing & Printing, Kokomo, IN. not paginated.
11. Grant County, Indiana obituaries & survivors, Vol. I, 18 Sep 1867 - 31 Dec 1894. Compiled 1986 by members of Grant County Genealogy Club. Selby Publishing & Printing, Kokomo, IN. 240 pp.
12. Grant County, Indiana obituaries & survivors, Vol. II, 1 Jan 1895 - 31 Dec 1897. Compiled 1986 by members of Grant County Genealogy Club. Selby Publishing & Printing, Kokomo, IN. 233 pp.
13. Grant County, Indiana obituaries & survivors, Vol. III, 1 Jan 1898 - 31 Dec 1900. Compiled 1987 by members of Grant County Genealogy Club. Selby Publishing & Printing, Kokomo, IN. 257 pp.

14. Grant County, Indiana obituaries & survivors, Vol. IV, 1
    Jan 1901 - 31 Dec 1904. Compiled 1987 by members of
    Grant County Genealogy Club. Selby Publishing &
    Printing, Kokomo, IN. 360 pp.
15. Grant County, Indiana marriage records, Vol. III, Mar
    1898 - Jan 1910. Compiled 1985 by members of Grant
    County Genealogy Club. Selby Publishing & Printing,
    Kokomo, IN. not paginated.
16. Grant County, Indiana marriage records, Vol. II, Apr 1882
    - Mar 1898. Compiled 1985 by members of Grant County
    Genealogy Club. Selby Publ. & Printing, Kokomo, IN.
    not paginated.
17. Hinshaw, W.W. 1978. Encyclopedia of American
    Quaker genealogy, Vol. I. Genealogical Publ. Co., Inc.,
    Baltimore, MD. 1,185 pp. + 12 pp. Errata & addenda.
18. Davis, E.A., and J.S. Ireton. 1981. Quaker records of the
    Miami Valley of Ohio. McDowell Publ., Utica, KY. 237
    pp. + errata and addenda + index.
19. Grant County, Indiana obituaries and survivors, Vol. V,
    1 Jan 1905 - 31 Dec 1907. Compiled 1989 by members of
    Grant County Genealogy Club. Selby Publ. & Printing,
    Kokomo, IN. 378 pp.
20. "Fairmount News," Microfilm, Fairmount Public
    Library, Fairmount, IN.
21. Area history of Fairmount, Indiana. 1997. Curtis Media,
    Inc. 414 pp.
22. Baldwin, E.M. 1917. The making of a township, Fair-
    mount Township, Grant County, Indiana 1829 to 1917.
    Edgar Baldwin Printing Co., Fairmount, IN. 503 pp.
23. History of Grant County, Indiana. 1886. Brant & Fuller,
    Chicago, IL. 895 pp.
24. Biographical memoirs of Grant County, Indiana. 1901.
    Bowen Publ. Co., Chicago, IL. 895 pp.
25. Whitson, R.L. 1914. Centennial history of Grant County,
    Indiana 1812 to 1912, Vol. 1 and Vol. 2. Lewis Publ.,
    Chicago, IL. 1,429 pp.
26. Harvey, H. 1925. History of Little Ridge Meeting.
    unpubl. typed manuscript. 8 pp.
27. Combination atlas map of Grant County, Indiana. 1877.

Kingman Brothers. 109 pp.

28. "Lest we forget," reminiscences of the pioneers of Grant County, Indiana. 1921. Marion High School History Dept. 148 pp.

29. Rhoades, G.E. 1994. Estates of Serenity, formerly I.O.O.F. Cemetery, Marion, Indiana, Vol. 1, A - K, pp. 1-172; Vol. 2, L - Z, pp. 173 - 342. Marion Public Library. looseleaf.

30. Hinshaw, W.W. 1994. Encyclopedia of American Quaker genealogy, Vol. V, Ohio. Genealogical Publ. Co., Baltimore. 1,060 pp.

31. Grant County, Indiana obituaries and survivors, Vol. VI, 1 Jan 1908 - 31 Dec 1910. Compiled 1991 by members of Grant County Genealogy Club. Selby Publ. & Printing, Kokomo, IN. 378 pp.

32. Grant County, Indiana obituaries and survivors, Vol. VII, 1 Jan 1911 - 31 Dec 1913. Compiled 1994 by members of Grant County Genealogy Club. Selby Publ. & Printing, Kokomo, IN. 276 pp.

33. Heiss, W. 1972. Abstracts of the Records of the Society of Friends in Indiana, Part Four. Indiana Historical Society, Indianapolis. 500 pp.

34. Heiss, W. 1975. Abstracts of the records of the Society of Friends in Indiana, Part Six. Indiana Historical Society, Indianapolis. 456 pp.

35. Grant County, Indiana marriage records, Vol. IV, Jan 1910 - Oct 1924. Compiled 1985 by members of Grant County Genealogy Club. Selby Publ. & Printing, Kokomo, IN. not paginated.

36. Grant County, Indiana marriage records, Vol. V, Oct 1924 - May 1938. Compiled 1985 by the members of Grant County Genealogy Club. Selby Publ. & Printing, Kokomo, IN. not paginated.

37. I.O.O.F. Cemetery, Marion, Grant County, Indiana interment record, Book I (A - J). Compiled 1977 by members of Grant County Genealogy Club, Marion, Indiana. 237 pp.

38. I.O.O.F. Cemetery records, Marion, Grant County, Indiana, Book II (K - Z). Compiled 1977 by members of Grant County Genealogy Club, Marion, Indiana. 280 pp.

39. Grant County, Indiana obituaries and survivors, Vol. 10,
    1935 - 1936. Compiled 1977 by members of Grant County
    Genealogy Club. Selby Publ. & Printing, Kokomo, IN.
    272 pp.
40. Grant County, Indiana obituaries and survivors, Vol. 9,
    1932 - 1934. Compiled 1996 by members of Grant County
    Genealogy Club. Selby Publ. & Printing, Kokomo, IN.
    not paginated.
41. Kirkpatrick, R.D. 1997. Local history and genealogy
    abstracts from "Fairmount News," Fairmount, Indiana
    1888 - 1900. Heritage Books, Inc., Bowie, MD. 158 pp.
42. Kirkpatrick, R.D. 1996. Local history and genealogical
    abstracts from Jonesboro and Gas City, Indiana
    newspapers 1889 - 1920. Heritage Books, Inc., Bowie,
    MD. 247 pp.
43. Thomas, J., and D. Roe. 1988. Grant County, Indiana
    connections. Selby Publ. & Printing, Kokomo, IN.
    334 pp.
44. Whitson, R.L. June 1903 - January 1905. Countryside
    and wayside. Marion Leader Tribune. Copied 1989 by
    L.W. Adams for Marion, Indiana Public Library. 130 pp.
45. Baldwin, F.C. 1985. The Baldwins from Virginia
    westward. publ. by author, Oak Park, IL. 141 pp.
46. Family genealogies, census records. Submitted by
    various persons for the collections of Marion Public
    Library, Marion, IN.
47. Kientz, M.A., comp. 1996. Grant County, Indiana Index
    of Deaths, 1888 - 1903, Grant County Books 1 - 4.
    Looseleaf in collections of Marion Public Library,
    Marion, IN. not paginated.
48. Kientz, M.A., copier. 1994. Burial records of Parrill &
    Lewis Funeral Home, Fairmount, Indiana. Collections
    of Marion Public Library, Marion, IN. 224 pp.
49. Handwritten minutes of Deer Creek Monthly Meeting of
    Anti-Slavery Friends. Photocopy in collections of
    Marion Public Library, Marion, IN. not paginated.
50. 1860 United States Census Records for the State of
    Indiana.
51. Adams, L., and W. Ratliff, copiers & indexers. 1887.

Probate records, Grant County, Indiana. Probate Book A (1831-1846). Volume 1 (Sept 1831-Aug 1841). Marion Public Library, Marion, IN. 270 pp.

52. Adams, L., *et al.*, abstracters. 1988. Grant County probate records, Marion, Indiana. Vol. 2 (Feb term 1842-Aug. term 1847). Marion Public Library, Marion, IN. 73 pp.

53. Will records, Grant County, Indiana Books A & 1 through 6. typed by M.A. Kientz from records of the Grant County Genealogy Club & the D.A.R-Kendall records. Looseleaf in collections of Marion Public Library, Marion, IN. 132 pp.

54. Rhoades, G., comp. 1992. Grant County, Indiana 1870 Census index. Marion Public Library, Marion. 57 pp.

55. Young, A.W. 1872. History of Wayne County, Indiana. Robert Clarke & Co., Printers, Cincinnati. 459 pp.

56. Kirkpatrick, R.D. 1998. Local history and genealogical abstracts from the Fairmount News 1901 - 1905. Heritage Books, Inc., Bowie, MD. 175 pp.

57. Blinn, K.E., comp. 1985. Marion in the mirror: a scrapbook of Rose B. Marsh clippings (from Marion, Indiana newspapers). 149 pp. Looseleaf in collections of Marion Public Library, Marion, IN.

58. Obituaries from Marion, Indiana Newspapers 1914 - 1931. Copied by members of the Grant County, Indiana Genealogy Club. Deposited in files of Grant County, Indiana Genealogy Club.

59. Heavilin, M.W. Not dated. Handwritten Genealogy Records. Deposited in the files of the Grant County, Indiana Genealogy Club.

60. American Annual Monitor....or Obituary of the members of the Society of Friends in America.... Tract Assoc. of Friends, New York. Numbers 1-6. 1858-1863.

61. Heiss, J.R., abstractor & comp. 1974. Obituary notices in the Christian Worker: a Quaker periodical 1874-1894. 2 vols. 285 pp. Bound typewritten copy deposited in collections of Earlham College, Richmond, IN.

62. Friends Review. Philadelphia, PA. Volumes 2-19, 1848-1866.

63. pers. comm., Thomas D. Hamm. August 26, 1998.

64. Deer Creek Monthly Meeting of Friends Birth and Death Record Book. Photocopy of original handwritten copy deposited in Marion Public Library, Marion, IN.
65. Mississinewa Monthly Meeting of Friends Birth and Death Record Book A. Photocopy of original hand-written copy deposited in Marion Public Library,
66. pers. comm., Rosemary (Wright) Matchette. August 31, 1998.
67. pers. comm., Carl A. Brookshire. August 31, 1998.
68. pers. comm., Jackie C. (Penrod) Thomas. September 23, 1998.
69. pers. comm., Meta (Carey) Turner. September 22, 1998.
70. Ridlen, C.A., compiler. 1979. Henry County, Indiana Early Marriage Records 1823-1839. no listed publisher. 43 pp.
71. Brien, L.M., compiler. 1935. Miami Valley Records, Vol. VI, Quaker Records. reprinted 1986 by Miami Valley Genealogical Society. 121 pp.
72. Selby, R.E., and P.J. Selby. 1981. Wayne County, Indiana Marriage Records 1811 - 1830. Selby Publ. & Printing, Kokomo, IN. 61 pp.
73. Grant County and Who's Who. 1909. reprinted 1988 by Selby Publ. & Printing, Kokomo, IN. 86 pp.

ABBOT, Alice 27
ACHOR, Sarah 121
ADDINGTON, Hannah 71 Mary Martha 80
ADKIN, Margaret 97
ALBRIGHT, Mary 72
ALLEN, Esther 96
ANDREW, Amanda 88 Lydia 113
ANDREWS, Hannah 2
ARNETT, Anna 112 Annis 126 Elmina 123 126
    Mahala 127 Thirza 118
AVERMON, Leona 35 44
BALDWIN, Abigail 59 124 Charlotte 18 114 Emily
    55 Mary 8 49 Milly 6 14 Pelinia 87
    Susannah 63
BALES, Sarah 108
BALLINGER, Anna 123 Sarah 31
BEA(L)L(E)S, Elizabeth 4 Mahala 94 Margaret 127
    Sarah 103 115
BECKERDITE, Elizabeth 106
BEEMAN, Penina 123
BENBOW, Jane 48 Miriam 50
BETTY, Rachel 30 86
BISHOP, Angeline 120
BOGUE, Anna 14 Elmina 93
BOND, Ann 19 Flora 4 Mary 93
BOUSSAN, Disa Belle 69
BOWEN, Jane 70
BOXELL, Nancy Jane 17 71
BOYD, Isabelle 96
BREWER, Cynthia Anna 67 Rosa 103
BRIGHTWELL, Elizabeth 114
BRISTENDINE, Lucinda 17
BROOKS, Hannah 88
BULLER, Mary 6 12
BUNDY, Lydia 71 Mirium 32
BURFORD, Mary 35
BURK, Lavina 102
BURNES, Elizabeth 87
BURROUGH, Patience 40

BURSON, Mahala   19
BUTLER, Michel   9   Tacy   49
CABE, Mary   28
CAIN, Ida May   48
CALDWELL, Frances   105
CAMMACK, Arsula   25   Mary   26   Rosella   60
CAMPBELL, Flora   37
CANADA(Y), Elizabeth   15   Margaret   73   Mildred   69
CAREY, Hannah   121   Ruth   121   Sarah   34   118
   Susannah   126
CARREL, Mary   16
CARROLL, Kate   50   Samira   97
CARTER, Edna   25   Elizabeth   104   Lydia   41   Martha
   6   Mary   8
CERTAIN, Wren   96
CHAMNESS, Mary   44   98
CHANEY, Emma   30
CHARLES, Elizabeth   98
CHEW, Hannah   26   Mary   41
CHOPSON/CHOPSIN, Margaret   122
CLARK, Mary   121   Molly   40   Paulina   26   Sarah   56
   104   118
CLEARWATER, Anna   88
CLOUD, Bertha   23
COATS, Esther   83
COFFIN, Caroline   36   Eva   55   Mourning   84
COGGESHALL, Ann(a)   18   36   Gulia   52   Hannah   107
   Lucy   7   Mary   7   38   Mary Della   12   Millicent
   30
COLEMAN, Harriet   67   98
COMPTON, Mary   86
CONNER, Mary   4   50   Sarah Ann   63
COOK, Charity   96   Hannah   32   Mary   121   Penina   10
COOPER, Mary   85   Rhoda   4   38
COPPOCK, Jane   33
CORNELIUS, Elizabeth   10
COX, Ann   105   120   Guelma Julia   125   Hannah   68
   78   Martha   127   Minnie   30   Nancy   70   Rebecca
   51

CRANDALL, Martha   74
CURTIS, Amanda   36
DAMERON, Catherine   96
DAVIS, Elizabeth   126   Ida   88   Mary   94   98   114
   Rhoda   38
DOAN, Rachel   112
DOHERTY, Nancy Ellen   20
DOUGLAS, Sarah   22
DRAPER, Elizabeth   48   70   Malinda   57   Millicent   45
   Miriam   57
DRUCKEMILLER, C. 'Polly'   28
DUNBAR, Mary   120
DUNCAN, Rachel   123
EDGEL, Sarah   89
EDGERTON, Cynthia   32   Mary   40
EILER, Elizabeth   10
ELLIOTT, Catharine   5   49   Elizabeth Jane   119   Johanna
   13   Lydia   77   Malinda   88   Margaret   99   Sara
   86
ELLIS, Nancy   30   36   39
EMBREE, Mary   123
ENGLE, Ida   37
ESHERMAN/ESHELMAN, Anna   66
EVANS, Ann   39   Mary   4   Sarah   75
FARIS, Elizabeth   126
FARMER, Catharine   19
FAULKNER, Ellen   2
FAUST, Frances   120
FENSTE(R)MAKER, Marie   3   Sarah Ella   42
FISHER, Rebecca Anna   84
FORBES, Catherine   29
FRAZZEE, Laura   2
FULKERSON, Delilah   65
FULTON, Harriet   112
GARDNER, Elizabeth   7   15   Luella   80
GARNER, Rhoda   15   Ruth   113
GIBSON, Mary   23
GORDON, Mahala   38
GOSSETT, Keziah   9

GREEN, Hannah 85 Margaret 112 Sarah Emma 70
GRIFFIN, Sarah 60
GUYER, Rebecca 69 98
HADLEY, Carrie 49 Ruth 104 117 Zilpha 103
HAINES, Helen 62 Louise 11
HAISLEY, Anzonetta 38 118 Caroline 119 Eunice 84
    Jane 10 11 112 Mary 111 122 Phoebe 113
    118 124 Sarah 113 Susanna 127
HALE, Dorcas 124 Nancy 125
HALL, Elizabeth 54 Eunice 80 Mary 66 Miriam 87
HALLENBACK, Mary 61
HAMMOND, Viola 61
HARLEN, Nancy 48 82
HARMON, Elizabeth 19 Irene 80
HARRELL, Lucinda 50
HARRIS, Chloe 93 Katherine 10 Maris 52 97 123
    Mary Alice 38 Nellie 94 Rachel 39
HARROLD, Leah 122 Mary 122 Rachel 6
HARTER, Massey 60
HARVEY, Keziah 97 Mary 106 Rebecca 102 Sarah
    104
HASTING, Mossie 102
HATHAWAY, Carrie 66 Jennie 68
HAWKINS, Ann/Anna 10 28 116 Hannah 116
HENLEY, Jane 68
HIATT, Elizabeth 48 Hannah 44 Jane 21 Minerva
    13 Nancy 20 Rachel 72 Susanna(h) 27 38
HIGGINS, Isabella 96
HIGHFIELD, Mary 102
HITE, Harriet 108
HIX, Belle 63
HOBSON, Asenath 114
HOCKETT, Alvina 32 77 Elizabeth 105 122 Emily 7
    Eunice 87
HODGIN, Abigail 6 Elizabeth 53 Martha 84
HODSON, Emma 94
HOGIN, Emily Elizabeth 44
HOLDEN, Susanna 9

HOLLINGSWORTH, Charity 59 Della 64 Elizabeth 64
   77 107 Lydia 37 94
HOLLOWAY, Ruth 112
HOLMES, Nancy 64
HOOVER, Rachel 104
HORN, Eliza 59 Elizabeth 2
HORTON, Rachel 127
HOWARD, Caroline 97 Mary 4
HOWELL, Catharine 74
HUMBLE, Grace 9
HUNT, Amy 48 Rachel 94
HUTCHINS, Amanda 53 Anna 33
JACKSON, Elsie 77 Emily 10 Olive 92
JANNEY, Patience 36
JAY, Anna May 13 Charity 4 Evangeline 19 Gulie
   67 Mary 4 53 Sarah 10 Susan 63
JESSUP, Sarah 34 118
JOHNSON, Martha 15 Rachel 65 Sarah 75
JONES, Aladelpha 2 Caroline 124 Eleanor 111 121
   Elizabeth 54 Esther 18 Huldah 32 Ida 126
   Jemima 71 Lucy 26 Lydia 33 Margaret 51
   Martha 55 Mary 57 Phebe 65 Rebecca 74
JORDAN, Flora 37
KANNARD, Myrtle 47
KELL(E)Y, Abigail 115 Emily 3 Lottie 93
KENDALL, Elizabeth 61 Ruth 117
KENNEDY, Elizabeth 16 38
KENYON, Hannah 60
KIMBROUGH, Elizabeth 118
KING, Martha 77 Sarah 54
KIRK, Mary 120
KNIGHT, Beulah 40 Elizabeth 11 63 Emma 62
   Lucinda 34 Mary 17 Nora 52 Sarah 84
KRIM, Elizabeth Alice 67
LACEY, Caroline 76 Eliza 31
LAMB, Catherine 24 Rebecca 13
LAMM, Sarah 13
LARRENCE, Cyrena 34
LAWSON, Grace 12

LEAPLEY, Gertrude 60 Ida 50
LEVERTON, Anna Jane 76 Rachel 26
LINDSAY, Serina 64
LITTLER, Lydia 114
LLOYD, Elizabeth 61 Lorena 19 Sarah 6
LOCKHART, Narcissus 66
LOMAX, Nancy 82
LOVE, Elizabeth 34
LUCAS, Isabella 3 91
LYON, Rachel 65
McCLAREN, Margaret 4 15
McCORMICK, Anna 44
McCRACKEN, Ann 53 Asenith 99 Mary 14
McCRUM, Charity 92
McINTIRE, Hannah 32
McNAIR, Clara 30
McWILLIAMS, Martha 23
MACY, Mary 37
MANDFIELD, Margaret 114
MARINE, Ruth 98
MARSHALL, Mary 62 Rachel 112
MAYNARD, Cynthia 35
MEEKS, Jemima 46
MENDENHALL, Charity 5 Hannah 3 58 Sally 117
MEREDITH, Sarah 34
MICKEL, Laura 41
MILLER, Hannah 125 Leona 55 Mariah 120 Ocea
    36 Rebecca 16
MILLIKAN, Hannah 12
MILLS, Lydia 86 Mary 47 Sarah 59
MILNER, Mary 118
MODLIN, Charlotte 22 Mary 80 Penina 81 Sarah
    58 82
MOON, Elizabeth 112 Olive 117
MOORE, Almeda 43 Gracie 81 Ida 15 Jerusha 87
    Rachel 83
MOORMAN, Anna 6 Polly 58
MORGAN, Elizabeth 9 Hannah 41
MORRIS, Hannah 24 Milia 74 Sarah 87

MURRAY, Elizabeth   73   115   Mary   120
MUSGROVE, Sarah   50
MYERS, Elizabeth   85
NEAL, Sarah   128
NEEDDOM, Elizabeth   113
NELSON, Susan   22
NEWBERN, Lillie Gertrude   59
NEWBY, Almira   56   Mirium   70
OPPEY, Sarah Ann   44
OREN, Ruth   59
OSBORN, Abigail   68   97   Martha   10   26   Nancy   94
    Tamer   62
OSBUN, Sarah   81
OVERMAN, Elizabeth   77   Mary   49   115   Pheraba   83
    Rachel   25   74   Rebecca   117   Sarah   72
OWENS, Allie   92   Eva   95
PAGETT, Elizabeth   65
PAINTER, Berthenia   21
PARKER, Mary   14
PARSON, Catherine   72
PARSONS, Mary   17
PATTERSON, Mary   16
PAYNE, Charlotte   18   114
PEACOCK, Lavina   113
PEARSON, Anna   39   Hannah   40   Huldah   22   Mary
    32   75   Rebecca   21   Sarah   63
PEEBLES, Mary   32
PEEL(L)E, Rebecca   66   99   Sally   93   Sarah   48   67
PEMBERTON, Eunice   24   Jessie   34
PENROD, Rachel   28
PERISHO, Clarissa   71
PHIL(L)IPS, Ann   117   Luanna   57   Sarah   61
PIERCE, Elizabeth   28   Serena   108
PIGGOTT, Margery   78
POE, Nancy   43
POWELL, Mary   57
PRESNALL, Julia   51   Rachel   64
PRICE, Catherine   21   Emaline   43   Sarah   72   103
PRITCHETT, Laura   88

PUCKETT, Ann/Rosanna 92 95
PUGH, Precious 115
PURVIS, Sarah 16
PYEATTE, Ruth 46
RADLEY, Elizabeth 124
RANDALL, Ann 73 82 Elizabeth 42 Martha 74
RATLIFF, Hannah 19 Millicent 71 Sarah 68 98
REDENBAUGH, Matilda 65
REECE, Catharine 108 Charity 107
REEDER, Eleanor 127 Rebecca 103
RICE, Mary 4
RICH, Amanda 111 Dinah 124 Elmira 115 Jane
    121 Ruth 111 Sophia 128 Susannah 7
ROMINE, Louisa 23
ROSE, Matilda 17
RUE, Lydia 57
RUSH, Dorcas 120 Nettie 104
St. CLAIR, Phebe 35
SANDERS, Nancy 22
SAP, Hester 101
SCHOOLEY, Anna 76
SCOTT, Melinda 111
SEARS, Maria 37 Mary 7
SHERIDAN, Nancy Emma 88
SHIELDS, Arminta 53
SHUGART, Abigail 92 Elizabeth 70 Gulielma 15 30
    92 Henrietta 45 Josephine 26 Mary 52
    Mary 94 Rachel 21 Sarah 24 75 82 93
SIMPSON, Phebe 46
SIRK, Jennie 79
SKINNER, Corintha 74
SLEEPER, Avis 3 40
SLIGER, Ellen 67
SMALL, Elizabeth 39 Emma 17 Hulda 36 Lucy 75
    Mary 8 17 24 88 95 Rachel 25 54 69
    Ruth 16 Sarah 5 58 60 82
SMITH, Anna 7 Mary 57 71 Melissa 72 Sally 111
    Sarah 82
SNEAD, Lydia 51 79 Mary 35 Susanna 60 81

SNORF, Kittie   2
SOUTHWORTH, Emma   78
STAFFORD, Julia   67
STALKER, Paulina   86
STALLINGS, Sarah   58
STANFIELD, Lydia Jane   4
STANLEY, Margaret   34   Martha   73
STANTON, Elizabeth   125
STARBUCK, Ann   26
STEED, Martha   52
STEVENS, Matilda   17
STOTT, Arrilla Matilda   46
STOUT, Elma   77   Mary   59
STRATTON, Letitia   10   28   Sarah   87
STUBBS, Keziah   117
SULGROVE, Elizabeth   20   31   44
SULLIVAN, Margaret   31
SYMON(D)S, Elizabeth   2   Jane   9   27   70   Sarah   1
TALBOT, Rebecca   57   123
TAYLOR, Lydia   5
THARP, Elizabeth   93   Harriet   3   Ruth   8
THOMAS, Celia   76   Christian   42   Cliffie   42   Emily
     33   45   64   Gulielma   6   Hannah   32   Huldah   9
     63   84   89   Jane   85   Lucinda   13   Lydia   3   91
     Martha   31   Mary   64   68   73   Minerva   81
     Nancy   51   Polly   58   74   Rhoda   37   Ruth   51
     Susannah   47   60
THORNBURGH, Emma   88
TRADER, Eunice   103
TROWBRIDGE, Viola   74
TURNER, Rebecca   97
VanCANNON, Julie   16
VICKERY, Dorcas   106
VOTAW, Jane   76
WARD, June   81
WAREHAM, Eliza   37
WATKINS, Ruth   23
WAY, Martha   81   Rachel   81   99
WEASNER, Nancy   34

WEESNER, Lacy/Lucy 5 42
WELCH, Elizabeth 54 Julia 17
WELLS, Eliza 101 105
WHISLER, Mary 6
WHITE, Margaret 17 Mary 106
WHITSON, Ann 66 Phebe 13 92
WIANT, Elizabeth 85 Rachel 30 38 Susannah 42
WICKERSHAM, Lydia 16
WIL(L)CUT(T)S, Christian 3 Elizabeth 47 Martha 41
    Melissa 80 Rachel 41 84
WILLIAMS, Emma 113 116 Margaret 126
WILSON, Lucy 106 Nancy 15 20 Olga 45 Ruth 24
WINSLOW, Anna 111 125 Martha 68 Mirium 113
    127 Sarah 105
WOODY, Effie 52
WROE, Arminta 65
WRIGHT, Anna 6 Hannah 43 Isabella 56 Malinda
    105 Phebe 106 Rachel 104
YATES, Grace 9
YATES, Minnie Maria 74
YOUNG, Elizabeth 101 Sarah 106
ZENTMEYER, Hannah 107

Other Heritage Books by Ralph D. Kirkpatrick, Ph.D.

Back Creek Friends Cemetery Burial Records
Revised Edition

Burial Records of Four Grant County, Indiana
Quaker Cemeteries

Local History and Genealogy Abstracts from
Fairmount News, *Fairmount, Indiana, 1888–1900*

Local History and Genealogy Abstracts from
Fairmount News, *Fairmount, Indiana, 1901–1905*

Local History and Genealogical Abstracts from
Jonesboro and Gas City, Indiana Newspapers, 1889–1920

Local History and Genealogy Abstracts from
Marion, Indiana Newspapers, 1865–1870

Local History and Genealogy Abstracts from
Marion, Indiana Newspapers, 1871–1875

Local History and Genealogy Abstracts from
Marion, Indiana Newspapers, 1876–1880

Local History and Genealogy Abstracts from
Marion, Indiana Newspapers, 1881–1885

Local History and Genealogical Abstracts from
Upland, Indiana Newspapers, 1891–1901

www.ingramcontent.com/pod-product-compliance
Lightning Source LLC
Chambersburg PA
CBHW071754090426

42737CB00012B/1814

* 9 780788 411182 *